C000253154

I AM HOPE

I AM HOPE

GROWING UP WITH AN ADDICT

STEPHEN HOPE

HOUNDSTOOTH
PRESS

COPYRIGHT © 2024 STEPHEN HOPE

All rights reserved.

I AM HOPE

Growing up With an Addict

FIRST EDITION

ISBN   978-1-5445-4532-5   *Hardcover*

978-1-5445-4531-8   *Paperback*

978-1-5445-4530-1   *Ebook*

This is a work of fiction. Any resemblance to actual people, living or dead, or places, names, companies, or incidents is entirely coincidental.

CONTENTS

INTRODUCTION

MY MOTHER'S DRUG ADDICTION WAS MY PROBLEM TOO. I was lost growing up. I stuttered. I was overweight. I was bullied, and I had no self-esteem. I felt like a burden to everyone. Being in that state of mind restricted my growth as a person. I was paralyzed by my surroundings. I didn't see any chance for escape. Every bit of light and happiness in life was drowned out by my mother and her addiction. As a child, I looked to the people raising me for guidance, and it took a long time to figure out they didn't have my best interests in mind.

If you were raised by an addict, or experienced other significant trauma in your childhood, you have likely experienced similar issues. This kind of childhood trauma is long lasting and forever affects the way you operate in life. Perhaps, like me, you struggle with confidence, trust, and the constant battle of life. Perhaps you are prone to mental illness, like depression or anxiety, as I am. You might be discouraged and wonder if you will ever recover and live a happy, healthy life. The good news, and perhaps also in some ways the bad news, is that the choice of where your life goes from here is yours and yours alone.

In the aftermath of an injury I'll describe in detail later, I learned I had a reason to live. Through one parent kicking me out for a new wife and the other being strung out on meth, I realized my parents were never going to prioritize me; it was up to me to look out for my own best interests. I recognized that if I were going to do anything significant with my life, I needed to establish a new direction in the crazy world in which I was living. I wish I could say that epiphany changed everything and I have lived happily ever after since, but of course, that's not how it works. Just as physical injuries create scar tissue, trauma creates emotional and mental scars. Learning how to deal and cope with my harmful past has been a journey, one that I'll work on for a lifetime. I began to use diet and exercise to strengthen both my mind and body. I reached out to a few people in my life for help. I shared my vulnerabilities with friends I trusted. Slowly but surely, I began to heal.

I will take you through my life from the scared, sad little boy I was to the confident, genuinely happy person I am today. I will show you the damage addiction does to a family. I will admit to the mistakes I made and acknowledge what I learned from them. I will share with you strategies and practices that helped me along the way. I will also introduce you to the book that drastically improved my life by opening the door between nutrition and mental health.

Throughout my journey, I read several books written by authors who experienced circumstances similar to mine. These books helped me through difficult times and inspired me. Just as the authors of those books made themselves vulnerable for the sake of helping others, I wrote this book to share my story and inspire you. My intent is not to tell you exactly what to do to improve your life—only you can determine what works for you—but my hope is that my story provides a glimpse into the cycle of addiction and a resource to help end it. I want you to know there is hope.

I am hope.

CHAPTER 1

THE ADDICT IN THE ROOM

I WAS RAISED BY A SINGLE MOM. SHE AND MY FATHER separated when I was a baby. She remarried several times and dated often, but those relationships didn't last. As a single parent, life was hard enough for her, but when she developed a drug addiction, raising me became nearly impossible.

What makes an addict? Addiction is all about escape. It can start off innocently, perhaps with an injured knee or back that requires drugs to escape from the pain. Eventually, your injury heals, but you keep using the drugs. Or maybe you were dealt a shitty hand in life and just want to escape reality for a moment. But life keeps knocking you down, and so you continue using those vices. The more you use those vices, the bigger the hold it has on your body and mind. Your body physically yearns for the next fix. You might swear it will be the last time, but in that moment, you choose drugs over everything else. It's a downward spiral, and gravity pulls more strongly the deeper you go. You start out using drugs as an escape, but the escape eventually becomes your permanent reality.

One unfortunate side effect of addiction is that the people close to the addict—friends, family, children—get chained to the addiction as well. When it becomes too hard to watch the addict self-destruct and refuse help, some friends and family remove themselves from the addict's life. But the child of an addict is stuck. I should know; I was that kid. I could not remove myself from the environment my mother created. My mother's life and mine were hopelessly intertwined. I was a victim of circumstance. I felt like the only way to escape my situation was to end my life. I believe my mom was aware of my depression, but since she wasn't able to care for herself, caring for me was impossible. Drugs always pulled her back in; her priority was the addiction.

CHAPTER 2

LIFE WITH MOM

WHEN I WAS VERY YOUNG, MY MOTHER WORKED AT JONES Carpet, a business owned and operated by my grandfather, Grandpa Jones. The warehouse was huge. I loved it. I could run around and get lost inside. I would sneak between large rolls of carpet, hanging out with or annoying the workers, depending on whom you asked. Plus, almost everyone there was family or felt like family. The carpet store became a safe place for me, a place I could go after school to escape my mom's crosshairs. Even though Mom always complained about working for Grandpa—I'm sure working with her father, aunts, uncles, and brother could be frustrating—I believe working there kept her grounded. I believe things started spiraling out of control when she quit because she no longer had family holding her accountable each day. She never kept a steady job again. Leaving that environment was heartbreaking for me. I missed being around my extended family most days.

Me before drug addiction completely consumed my mother's life.

Around this time, Mom's marriage to a man named Larry ended. Having him around helped us feel like we were a family, complete with a dog. We made some good memories together. Larry and I planted a row of pine trees behind our house. He took me camping and even let me bring my good friend Noah.

Things were normal until they weren't. Larry's violent side always bubbled just below the surface. I constantly heard Larry and Mom arguing, but Mom shielded me from it the best she could.

Then one day, Larry seemed to lose his mind. He went into a rage and decided to rearrange the house while Mom and I hid in the basement. I remember being scared out of my mind and hearing the VCR break. Mom made the right choice and ended it with Larry, but I was torn. I didn't like the arguing, but he kind of evened everything out and seemed normal most of the time. I know it had to be hard being a single mom, and Larry must have relieved some of the burden. Unfortunately, once Larry was gone, I was the one Mom screamed at all the time.

Josh, Gunner, and me at Josh's parents' for a cookout.

Mom's next husband was Josh, a good ol' boy. He drove a jacked-up Chevy Blazer with a sound system that nearly blew the windows out. The SUV was so high off the ground I could barely climb into the back seat. Mom and I hung out with his family. We all went fishing, and I thought everything was calm and back to normal. Josh laughed when I told him how much I liked him being around because Mom took her frustrations out on him instead of me. But then Mom started *really* fighting with him. She yelled and told him he was lazy. She hollered at him about how she carried the family without his help. I don't know if any of what she said was true or not. All I know is their marriage ended soon after the yelling started.

After Josh left, Mom brought home the occasional boyfriend. Every time a boyfriend or husband would leave, he would tell me, "You're the man of the house now." I didn't know what that meant at the time, but I learned to hate the phrase. It scared me.

Having new people live with us off and on came to feel normal. The part that never felt normal, that always hurt, was overhearing my mom talk about me to her friends in the bathroom, which was right next to my room, when I was supposed to be asleep. Often, she told them I was fat or complained that having me ruined her life. I liked to tell myself she was just drunk and rambling to her friends, but it still stung. I hated hearing how negatively I affected her life. Hearing that over and over was one thing, but I also could sense her feeling that I was only a burden to her life. The drunken nights got worse and more frequent after she stopped working at Jones Carpet. It didn't help that we lived within walking distance of the Days Inn Bar. Sometimes, she got so drunk her friends had to carry her home from the bar. I would run to the door, excited to see them until I saw my mom, incoherent and unable to stand or talk. I would ask if she was okay. Her friends would tell me someone slipped something into her drink or she just had a few too many and assure me she'd be fine.

Eventually, Mom moved into the basement and stayed there

most of the time. She made frequent trips to bars and brought back random people. I'll never forget Dirt, one of the guys she brought home from the bar. He had played in the band at the bar that night. He had dark, curly hair and dark clothing. I met them when they stumbled in through the kitchen's back door, which led down to the basement. Mom introduced him, beaming with pride that he had come home with her. They continued their path down the stairs and slammed the door behind them. I walked back to my room alone and got myself ready for bed.

※ ※ ※

Jobs came and went for Mom. She could never show up on time. Our financial situation got worse and worse. Eventually, she was put on watch lists at the local grocery stores for constantly writing bad checks. When she tried to check out, we'd have to see a manager or go to the front desk. That game only lasted so long before everyone in our small town figured out Mom was writing cold checks.

My grandfather frequently stepped in and helped us out financially. He paid for nearly everything for a good chunk of my childhood. Despite his generosity, my grandfather and my mom always got into shouting matches. Mom would rush us out of his house, complaining the whole car ride home about how awful he was. She would call him "manipulative" and "unhelpful." Then, she'd look at me and shout, "He's always trying to run my life!" I would sit in the passenger seat, trembling while feeling scared and afraid. I couldn't get away from her, so I would sink down as far as possible into my seat, trying not to draw any attention to myself.

Criticizing the people I loved and looked up to was normal behavior for my mother. If I said something positive about my dad or she saw me enjoying the time I spent with him every other weekend, she would tell me he was a manipulator and that he took drugs. She shared with me any piece of dirt she knew about him, true or not. I would protest and tell her she didn't really know him, but my words fell on deaf ears. However, I was naive about him as well.

Mom was the same way with her brother, Uncle Noah, whom I admired. He and his wife, Grace, were very successful in my eyes. They often took care of me when I was little. After spending a day at Noah's place or attending a family gathering, I'd try to tell my mom about the fun things I did with Noah. Her response was always the same: "You don't know him. He's lazy, he's a hypocrite, and he was a gambling addict." She also called him a "manipulator," like she did everyone in her life who wasn't a drinking buddy.

Another frequent presence in my life as a child was my grandmother. Mom often talked bad about her too, which confused me because they seemed so close and so similar. Mom would tell me about how Grandma used to whore around and that she was addicted to drugs, referring to my grandmother's prescription pills. And, of course, Mom accused her of being a manipulator. Mom's rantings discredited and cast a shadow over everyone I looked up to in my eyes. This took quite a mental and emotional toll on me, especially since I was a stuttering, fat, dumb kid and Mom's punching bag.

Despite my mother's ingratitude, my grandfather still tried to set me up for a better future. He paid for me to attend a private elementary school for four years, starting in third grade. My first year was a bit of an adjustment, but it wasn't bad. I made new friends, and I liked going to school there. It was a Catholic school, and they required me to be baptized. I had to do extra work after school to fulfill the baptism requirements.

Everything seemed to be going great. I had good grades, and my name was even in the newspaper for being on the honor roll.

Then, at the end of the school year, I was told to attend summer school or repeat the third grade. It didn't make sense. The schoolwork wasn't that hard, and the only complaint I had received from teachers was that I often finished my work early and talked to other students in class. They claimed I had a hard time getting my grades, but I felt that was absolute bullshit.

It was hard enough transferring to a new school and making new friends. Now, all those friends were moving on, while I had to repeat the entire process. The strain of trying to fit in with a new, younger group of kids was going to be tough. I already felt like I stood out because of my weight and stuttering, but adding being remedial from being held back a grade made fitting in impossible.

In my second year of third grade, I had the same teacher from one of my classes the previous year as my main teacher. She had seemed really nice in that one class so I thought that was positive. However, by the time classes started, my weight had ballooned and my stutter had become significantly worse. I could barely get a sentence out when called on. I tried different tricks to help with my stutter, such as drawing a square with my finger while talking. They helped but didn't cure the issue. My teacher took my stutter as a sign of a lack of intelligence on my part and an inconvenience to her class. Her solution was to put me in special classes. This ramped up my fear of being unintelligent and standing out. Making new friends in these circumstances felt hopeless. My weight and stutter continued to worsen.

My new special class consisted of me, a boy who had lost his mom, a boy who hated to talk, a super hyper kid, and two to three other students, who were all on the spectrum, depending on the day. Excluding the kids on the spectrum, the one thing we all shared was we were poor compared to the "normal" kids. I suspect we would have been treated differently if our parents had a higher financial status.

Ms. J was our special-class teacher. She was extremely nice and patient with everyone, but the classwork was too simple. It put me further behind the normal students. I bounced between the normal and special classes and found it much more difficult to understand what was going on in the normal class than I had before being enrolled in the special class. The normal students were learning at a faster pace than those of us in the special class, and I was falling behind. I began to accept that I was different and had an intellectual deficit compared to normal kids.

My belief in my own mental inferiority manifested itself in many ways throughout my school years. For example, I lost interest in the accelerated reading club at my school. In this club, each student read a book, was tested on it in the computer lab, and received points for every correct answer. At certain times throughout the year, students who had earned enough points during that period could attend a pizza or Coke party. In my first year at the school, I had more than enough points to participate in every party because I enjoyed reading and always understood what I read. But after being held back a year, I slowly stopped reading. I lost interest and thought, *I'm dumb. Why waste my time? Who cares? Why hone a skill with insufficient tools?* It wasn't until my sophomore year in college that I realized I had a normal mental capacity and could keep up with the students around me.

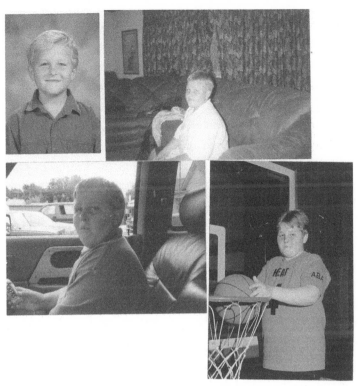

My transformation as drug addiction took over my mom's life.

This was a prime example of me letting society tell me who I was and dictate my value. I had already learned to normalize things in my environment that didn't make a lot of sense. The special classes added to my confusion, but I never thought to disagree. Instead, I let my circumstances change me. I couldn't blame my teachers because they didn't know we were going through a bankruptcy and losing our home. How could they know my mom was getting back from "vacation" (an extended stint in rehab)? How could they know I was being taken to a movie rental place in Spottsville, Kentucky, and waiting for hours in the car while my mom performed stripteases in the back of the place? How were they supposed to know or be able to do anything about it? What the teachers saw was a kid not performing to their standards, a kid with a horrible stutter who was interrupting their classes, talking during class, and acting like a class clown. I fell further behind in classwork as the year continued, and my interest in going to school and doing schoolwork faded fast. Even after I finished the year of remedial classes, began learning at the same pace as my classmates, and got back on the honor roll, I continued to act out in class and had very little interest in schoolwork.

In previous years, when I got home from school, Mom would help me study. We allotted a certain amount of time each night for it, and I would get stars if I completed all my homework. Once I earned a certain number of stars, she took me to McDonald's to get ice cream or somewhere else for a special treat. But the stronger my mom's addiction got, the less time she spent with me. Eventually, when I got home from school, I would simply go to my room to sleep, cry, or both and repeat the routine the next day.

Around this time, my mom went through bankruptcy and eventually lost our house. We moved into an apartment. The kids in the new neighborhood were brutal. To them, I was a stuttering, fat, preppy-looking kid: perfect prey. The older kids regularly jumped me on my way home from the bus stop. I tried to outrun them, but they were too fast, and I was outnumbered. As the bus approached my drop-off point, I would quietly move as close to the exit as possible. I needed every bit of a head start I could get. The best-case scenario was they would get distracted and forget about me. But most of the time, they started taunting me on the bus, and the closer we got to my stop, the louder they got. Once we got off and they started beating me, the best thing I could do was lie there until they lost interest and moved on. They rarely hit me in the face. Instead, they preferred to do wrestling moves on me. Once I was on the ground, they'd kick me then punch the back of my head while I was curled up into a ball.

I hated who I was. I hated my life. My weight tipped the scale at 220 pounds. I was a dumb, stuttering, blond-haired ball of fat, and on top of that, my mom thought I had ruined her life. All I wanted was to find some way out. What started as thoughts about running away quickly became much darker. Running away wouldn't solve the problem because *I* was the problem. Suicide[1] would be a vacation from this hell. I wouldn't have to worry about any of it anymore.

Once the thought of suicide entered my brain, it spread like a virus. It was all I could think about. I spent every spare minute alone in my room, and the solitude gave me plenty of time to think. I came up with four possible suicide methods: drowning, electrocution, burning, or hanging. After considering all four in great detail, I decided hanging was the best choice. I could use a rope or extension cord; either would work. Hanging could be my escape from this normal life.

The only thing that kept me from going through with my plans was feeling loved and knowing what my death would do to the ones who loved me. No matter how distant that love felt at times, I knew it was there. I could feel it. Words are just lip service. I judged people on their actions, and I knew my grandparents, dad, Uncle Noah, and Aunt Grace loved me.

When I was around nine years old, my mom had a fling with a wealthy man named Harrison. He was super nice to me. I remember taking a trip to Kentucky Lake with him. We spent

---

[1] If you or someone you know is experiencing suicidal thoughts, please reach out immediately to the Suicide and Crisis Lifeline at 988.

a really fun day riding inner tubes and fishing. Eventually, my mom became pregnant, even though Harrison had been told he was sterile. (In fact, a few years later, he got his new wife pregnant in the same month he had gotten my mom pregnant!) I'm not sure of everything that went on between Harrison and my mom during the pregnancy, but Mom circled around being normal. I think she quit some of her vices. A great memory I have from that time is sitting downstairs with her as she taught me how to crochet. Passing time with her like that was wonderful.

By the time my baby brother, Gunner, was born, Mom and Harrison's relationship had gone from bad to worse. Because she was a single mom, I did everything I could to help out. After a few months, Mom went back to staying locked in her room or bathroom all day and night, which left me figuring out how to take care of a small child. I learned how to do nearly everything for a baby. It was a great learning experience for me.

Me feeding Gunner Easter morning.

I was home alone with Gunner when he was two years old when I heard a knock at the door. When I opened it, I saw my grandmother Cathy, police officers, and some other people I didn't know. I was quickly shuffled to the side while they ambushed the apartment. They grabbed Gunner, and as quickly as they came in, they were gone. When the dust settled, I sat alone, confused and terrified.

Everyone thinks their childhood environment is normal. It's all we know. I had developed a stutter, become overweight, and started acting out in school. These should have been red flags for anyone paying attention, but my guardian was too high, or laid out after coming down from being high, to notice what I was going through. Though being frustrated by a parent is part of growing up, I always suspected something was off. However, when Child Protective Services took Gunner away, my suspicion became a reality. I knew something was seriously wrong. My mom was gone, my brother had been taken, my grandmother had gone with him, and I sat there alone. I remember wondering how everyone could have forgotten me. You don't know how naive you were as a child until you look back at the truth.

Gunner went to live with his father. Mom was allowed to see Gunner during supervised visits and then eventually without supervision one night a week and every other weekend. They also split holidays. I do not miss those trips to pick up or drop off Gunner at his dad's house. Most times Mom and Gunner's dad would argue on the front porch. Whether they did or didn't argue, I always got an earful. Mom would complain about Gunner's dad and stepmom, saying things similar to what she said about my dad, grandparents, uncle, and anyone else she had an opinion about. I was her dumping ground and had to absorb all her rage and negativity.

CHAPTER 3

LIFE WITH DAD

My dad returning me to my mother after spending the weekend with him.

MY DAD LIVED IN A THREE-BEDROOM, SINGLE-WIDE TRAILER on the other side of town with my stepmom and three sisters: an adopted older sister, a stepsister my age, and a younger half sister. My sisters and I were all regularly spanked, although my spankings were more frequent and intense than those suffered by my sisters. My stepmom spanked us the most, often using wooden spoons. When the spoons kept breaking, she began using a wooden paddle wrapped with black tape to keep it from cracking. That paddle hurt, but eventually, it broke too. Sometimes, she spanked us with her hand, when a paddle or spoon wasn't in arm's reach, but that stung her hand too much to be the norm.

Most of the time, my spankings were deserved. I was spanked for lying, for being mean to my sisters—for anything, really. Once, I was singing the lyrics to a Sawyer Brown song called "Thank God for You," which includes a line thanking the devil for the trouble the singer got into. That line infuriated my stepmom because she and her family were Roman Catholics who leaned into their religion; it was a constant in their lives. Naturally, being a bit of a shithead kid, I sang that part loudly. It didn't take too long for her to get mad enough to spank me. The reason that well-earned spanking sticks out in my mind is it felt like she was convinced the devil was inside me, forcing me to sing those lyrics around her strict, Roman Catholic family. It felt like she thought maybe she could beat the devil out of me. That made me think, *Maybe the devil* is *inside me.*

Despite being a shithead here and there, I felt some of the blame I received was unjustified. For instance, I was blamed for my stepsister Shannon breaking her arm, even though I wasn't there when it happened. On the weekends I visited my dad, I spent most of my time with Shannon, who was my age. One weekend, when we were hanging out together, I accidentally sat on her arm. When I arrived at my dad's place the following weekend, I learned Shannon had broken that same arm in a fall while playing outside a few days earlier. My stepmom blamed me, saying the significant pressure I put on Shannon's arm when I accidentally sat on it was what caused it to break later. This made me fear my weight even more than I already had. How could I unknowingly hurt one of my best friends? From then on, I was extremely hesitant when roughhousing with friends, fearing I could hurt them because of my weight.

Another incident that stands out in my mind involved a clothesline on the opposite side of our driveway, where Shannon and I often played. On this day, we tied a piece of rope to one of the clothesline poles and took turns swinging from it. We looped it around our waists or shoulders and spun around, hanging from the pole, swinging back and forth. On one of Shannon's turns, she looped the rope around her neck and swung back and forth. It was fascinating. I wondered, *How the hell is that not doing anything to her?* I asked her to do it again, but she said it hurt. I didn't want her to get hurt. I was just thinking about my plan to hang myself, and I felt more confused than ever. *How am I going to successfully hang myself if Shannon can swing around the clothesline from her neck completely unfazed?* I decided when I hanged myself, I needed something to kick out from under my feet so I wouldn't be able to save myself in a moment of weakness. Maybe the jolt would break my neck.

My brainstorming session was interrupted by my stepmom, who was ready to spank the shit out of me. She was mad at me for asking Shannon to swing from her neck again. My intention wasn't to hurt Shannon, but my stepmom didn't see it that way. She gave me a hard spanking, but I was confused by what I'd just seen, and my mind was somewhere else as she whaled on me.

My dad spanked me every now and then as well. His spankings were much less severe but much more hyped up. He would say he was going to get the belt with fishhooks that take flesh off with each strike. Let me be clear: that belt did not exist. It was just a scare tactic. However, his threats mixed with all the trash my mom would say about him made it hard for me to know how to feel toward him. There's no doubt I loved him, but I wondered whether or not he was a good person.

My dad and stepmom fought from time to time. I remember a few instances when they got into it pretty badly, with my stepmom telling us to call the cops while they crashed into each other in the trailer's hallway. My sisters and I were just scared kids. We didn't know what to do. We didn't actually call the police because who wants to call the cops on their parents? Plus, it looked like she was kicking his ass and well in control of the situation. They always seemed to make up shortly after these huge fights. At least, they did until they didn't.

My sisters and me. Youngest sister not pictured. She was not born yet.

Despite being spanked a lot at my dad's house, I preferred living with him to living with my mom. I hated the spankings at the time, but I do think that punishment, handed out so freely, helped overall. It balanced out my mom's approach, which was to do very little when it came to discipline, consequences, or paying attention. I asked my mom for years to let me live with my dad, and he tried to get full custody of me more than once. It seemed like my mom kept us kids to spite everyone else, which wasn't in anyone's best interest. She had other stuff going on and she dragged us through it all with her. By the time things were really bad with Mom, Dad was divorced. Living with him would have been such an improvement. I knew he wasn't perfect, but at least he admitted that. He told me about his past mistakes, which made him seem more human and approachable, not just an obstacle to be feared. I felt more comfortable around him.

The closest I ever came to living with my dad happened when I was eleven. I told him about a trip to Walmart where my mom searched the hunting section for something that could melt metal. She didn't hunt or fish, so it struck me as weird. I told my dad the thing she was looking for could be used to melt drugs. Dad arranged for a custody hearing, during which he retold the Walmart story, but not accurately. He either misunderstood my story or perhaps he wanted to misunderstand it. In his version of the story, I had witnessed my mom melting drugs. I'm sure he thought the only way I would suspect something like that at my age was if I had literally seen her do it. But during the hearing, when they asked me if I saw my mom use anything to melt down drugs, I told the truth: "No. I haven't." The only drug-related things I ever saw were her stash of weed and the paraphernalia she used to smoke it, but at that time, I didn't know weed was a drug, so I didn't mention it to the judge. Instead, I re-explained the Walmart shopping experience.

Though it was suspicious, it wasn't enough for my father to gain full custody.

CHAPTER 4

JUNIOR HIGH

FINDING FOOTBALL

THE SUMMER BEFORE I ENTERED SEVENTH GRADE, MY good friend Elrod told me football was starting up for junior high students, and he was going to play. If he was doing it, I was doing it. Football was hard, but at that age, I was pretty good. I played defensive end. Football provided physical activity, which helped me drop some weight, and it gave me a sense of purpose. The feeling of wanting to end my life started to drift away. The thoughts were still there, but they weren't as loud or urgent. I'm still proud of that first year; our team ended the season 10-0.

There is nothing like being part of a team. The structure of the practices and games and the feeling that my team was a family were just what I needed. The only downside was waiting for my mom to pick me up after practices and games. She was late nearly every time—sometimes ten minutes, sometimes several hours. Often, I sat and cried while I waited alone on the curb. I would call and suggest I get a ride with someone else, since there were at least three different teammates who lived within walking distance of our apartment, but she would say, "No, I'll be there." It was bullshit. Sitting and waiting for her to pick me up all those years, all alone, felt awful. And for what? I was scared and frustrated out of my mind. It was so damn unnecessary.

In addition to football, a highlight of those years was that since Gunner lived with his dad, I didn't have to take care of him. I had more free time, so I was able to spend more time at friends' houses and playing outside. Since Mom was in her own world, I got to do just about whatever I wanted, unless it inconvenienced her. For instance, when she got Gunner one night a week, we usually picked up fast food for dinner, and I had to take care of him while she locked herself in her room. Also, every other weekend, when it was her weekend with Gunner, I had to stay around the apartment to watch him while she went out, locked herself in her room, or locked herself in the bathroom.

During junior high, Mom began dating a guy named Cade. He had money, but he didn't have a good reputation. Mom told me he was rich, but he didn't dress like it. He was tall and slender with dark hair. Mom always mimicked the way he laughed. She looked up to him and did whatever he said. We moved to Robards, Kentucky, to live closer to Cade. He had a cabin in the woods on acres of land with a big lake to fish in. Luckily, I didn't have to switch schools. I really liked the house we moved into; it had an enclosed front porch that had been converted into an office area. If Cade didn't get the house for us, I think he at least played a big role in supporting Mom financially at that time. When we moved, Mom set up her room in the basement again, and I rarely saw her anymore.

Shortly after moving, Mom and Cade took a trip. I'm still

not sure exactly what happened, but they got caught with drugs. Once everything settled down, Cade took the fall for most of it, but Mom had to go back to rehab for the second time. She explained where she was going in some weird, vague way, as if it wasn't really rehab, and it made sense to me at the time. I stayed with my dad and grandparents while she was gone. When she was released from rehab a few months later, she bragged and boasted about how much fun it was. She told me someone dared one of the guys to grab her butt. It seemed like a game or joke to her. In my opinion, she had no intention of quitting anything. Rehab was a vacation for her.

After she was released from rehab, Grandpa Jones helped Mom get back on her feet. He bought her the house she still lives in today. Unfortunately, Mom was not grateful for the house nor what Grandpa did for us. She lashed out at him even more, accusing him of trying to run her life. I didn't want to hear it anymore, so I spent most of my time at other people's houses.

I remember the day my attitude toward my mom changed as clearly as if it were yesterday. I was fourteen years old, standing in the kitchen of our new house, and my friend JB was standing by the kitchen table. I told him I didn't respect my mom. I told him I loved her, but after waiting for her alone for hours after all those practices, after going through job loss after job loss with her because she could not show up on time, after being dragged through all that nonsense for no reason, and after hearing her say I ruined her life over and over again, I was done. It was just too much. Yet, despite realizing and acknowledging I had lost all respect for my mom, for some reason, at that time in my life, I still didn't think she used drugs or was a drug addict.

CHAPTER 5

JUNIOR YEAR OF HIGH SCHOOL

A LIFE-CHANGING INJURY

Mom, me, and Grandma Cathy at a dinner celebrating our football season.

BY THE TIME I WAS IN HIGH SCHOOL, MY WEIGHT HAD been an issue for a while. I had slimmed down from playing football, but the bullying and being called fat all my life had taken a toll; I still felt fat. No matter how I looked, I was never comfortable in my own skin. I stopped eating, even though I was still on the football team. My weight dropped from 187 pounds down into the 150s, but I still felt fat. I tried eating and throwing up afterward for a while because I didn't want people to notice I wasn't eating, but I hated the constant burning feeling in my throat. So, I tried simply not eating, and no one noticed. Starving myself was much better than eating and throwing up. Being as active as I was and not eating took a toll on my body. I had never broken a bone nor had a serious injury before, but the next thing I knew, I had broken a bone in my hand and separated my shoulder. My health issues finally came to a head when I passed out while standing around at my friend's house after we finished smoking some weed. By this time, I was smoking weed nearly every day. All the activity, stress, drugs, and lack of food were more than my body could take. My rigorous days and no calories didn't mix.

During my junior year of high school, after football season ended and my hand and shoulder healed, I started eating better and lifting weights. The guy who had played in front of me graduated, and I thought I had a chance to start as defensive end. I had a great routine and was the strongest I'd ever been (or will be). I made it into the eight-hundred-pound club, meaning that between my bench press, back squat, and power clean, I could lift more than eight hundred pounds. I thought injuries were a thing of the past.

To help with my training and workouts, I took supplements, which consisted mainly of Cell-Tech and whey protein. My body was performing great and adjusting to everything I was putting it through. When spring football hit, I reached my goal of being placed as the starting defensive end.

One day during practice, my position group was working with the linebackers. We lined up in two lines ten yards apart. One partner carried the ball, and the other partner tried to tackle him. As a starting defensive end, I was paired with one of the starting linebackers, Dustin Quinn. He was big, fast, and strong and would eventually become one of my closest friends. His best nickname was Missile, but I call him Quinn. The whistle blew, and we both ran as fast as we could, crashing into each other so hard we both stood straight up. Then, I collapsed to the side and started blacking out. My helmet was cracked on the right side, from my ear hole to the back of the helmet. At the time, I was young and dumb and didn't know exactly what had happened, so I just jumped up and got back in line to run the drill again. In line, I was blacking out, and my back began to hurt like I'd never felt before. My body must have been in shock, though, because the pain was bearable for the moment. I finished up practice and continued to hit like nothing had happened.

Everything is kind of a blur after that. I remember lying on the couch at home one second, and the next, I had so much back pain I could barely move. My head was also hurting badly. I told my mom I needed to go to the hospital. Once I got there, they ran tests but couldn't find anything wrong, so I got a new helmet and went back to practice with the intention of finishing the two weeks left of spring football. I toughed it out for a few days, but I ended up standing off to the side due to pain.

Once spring ball was over, I was still in severe pain, so I went back to the hospital. This time, they put me through a CAT scan machine and found subdural hematomas (bleeding) on the right side of my brain and herniated discs in my back.

Apparently, there had been so much swelling when they looked at me two weeks earlier they couldn't see any of the damage. They put me in a neck brace, placed me on a stretcher, and rolled me into a hospital room, where they pumped me full of pain meds.

Shortly after being released from the hospital, I went to see a back specialist for my herniated discs. He explained that when I hit Quinn at football practice, the impact compressed my back, causing the fluid sacs between three of my vertebrae to disappear into oblivion. The doctor said I was young enough that everything might heal. He also told me to be careful in everything I did and I shouldn't play football anymore.

After leaving the back specialist, I was pissed. I had worked so hard to put myself in a starting position on the football team during my senior year! I punched a stop sign as we walked to the car from the doctor's office. My mom, dad, grandpa, aunt, uncle, and several friends all told me it wasn't worth it to continue playing. What they didn't understand was that football was all I had. It was the only consistent thing in my life, and suddenly, it had been ripped away.

In hindsight, getting injured was one of the best things to ever happen to me. I finally put value on my life after this happened. I wanted something for myself; I had something worth fighting for. Football and the locker room were my safe places; my team was my family. What would I do without football? Spend more time at home? My home life was trash. I made the choice to not let my injuries affect the way I lived my life. That was the first time I made a decision strictly for me. It was a truly life-changing decision. Making that choice showed me I wanted to live for something in the future. I didn't want to live my life with no direction, just trying to survive or escaping each day. I had a purpose. It was not an extremely long-term goal, but it was a positive start: I was determined to return to football. I didn't know if that was actually possible, but I was going to do it or die trying. I blocked out all the outside noise and zoned in on getting my starting position back.

Having this new mindset changed everything. It pulled me away from that dark space where, until now, I'd spent so much time. A dark place is the best way I can describe where I felt during my lowest moments. The term "spiraling out of control" fits. I felt like I was orbiting a planet. The closer I was to the planet, the more centered or grounded I became. The farther I went into orbit, the darker it got. I would drift off into that dark space, where I felt all alone no matter how many people were around. I felt like a shell of a human being. Nothing got in, and nothing got out. My surroundings were lifeless. I lived in that place the majority of my childhood. I was depressed and suicidal. Even though I stopped eating and lost a significant amount of weight, no one noticed, except my girlfriend, who said I was too skinny. Thankfully, some things pulled me back into orbit occasionally, like knowing someone loved me, playing football, and having responsibilities. The dark feelings would temporarily go away, lying dormant until the right moment, when I would start to drift away again. But nothing was stronger than valuing my life. That is what really pulled me out of the darkness.

Making the choice to play football again might have been dumb physically, but it did wonders for me mentally. I suddenly valued something. I got serious about going to college and improved my attentiveness at school for the short term, which was another step in the right direction. I talked with my back specialist about rehab and how hard I could push it. Around late May, I started working out with light weights and doing light cardio. The herniated discs in my back caused pain when

I moved or did random activities, but the worst part was my subdural hematomas. I suffered severe migraines and was in constant pain for months. I would take twenty herniated discs before I'd go through another brain injury. It's ruthless; the pain doesn't stop. Imagine the worst migraine of your life, and then imagine living with it for months with no reprieve. That constant pain tries to break you. I still have headaches to this day, and I believe they are the result of my first brain injury. My plan was to do low-intensity workouts until I built enough strength to push myself further. I listened to my body. When my headache intensified, I backed off. When my back pain threatened to keep me from being able to work out again the following day, I backed off. Sometimes, I flirted on the edge of pushing too hard too early, and I lost time to recover. However, it was hard to be cautious when I didn't have an abundance of time. Football season was fast approaching, and if I wasn't able to practice, I wouldn't play that fall, much less start.

I worked out alone at our local YMCA three to five times a week. Time was tight with school, football, and work. About a month into my training, Duffy, the head football coach, told me if I could get back into the eight-hundred-pound club before school started, he'd give me my starting position back. That was the first time someone else recognized I could get back to playing football, and it was all the motivation I needed. He gave me hope, and hope is a powerful thing.

After that conversation, I centered my programming around getting back into the eight-hundred-pound club, which meant strengthening the muscles used for benching, power cleaning, and squatting. My injuries made progress slower than what I wanted, but I stayed consistent. I was laser focused on accomplishing my goal. With only a week or two left before school started, I was finally strong enough to lift the same amount of weight I could before the injuries. When I hit that goal, I gave a few high fives to the guys I was lifting with and an assistant coach and prepared to tell Coach Duffy. I was excited to tell him, though going into his office was always a little scary. I walked in and told him I just got back into the eight-hundred-pound club. He said, "Alright," and that was it. I kept my composure in the weight room, but when I walked out to the parking lot and got in my car, I couldn't stop crying. I was so happy. I had accomplished my goal in spite of everyone telling me it wasn't possible and my own fear they might be right.

CHAPTER 6

SENIOR YEAR OF HIGH SCHOOL

ON MY OWN

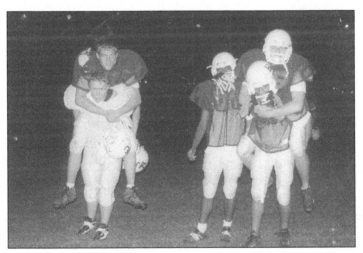

Me and a teammate being carried off the practice field our last day of football practice senior year.

MY SENIOR YEAR OF HIGH SCHOOL BEGAN WELL. I HAD regained my starting position and played well in the first two scrimmages leading into our first game of the season. I started the first four games. But having reached my goal of starting, I lost focus, and it showed in my play on the field. I fell into my old habits of smoking weed all the time and not being prepared. When I was focused on my goal, I didn't have time for those bad habits, but without a goal to focus on, I was just going through the motions. Then one day, I got rear-ended pulling out of a McDonald's on the way to practice, so I arrived late. I was demoted to second string. The coaches had been looking for an excuse to pull me from the starting position, and that was it. I don't blame them a bit. I stayed on second string, playing here and there for the rest of my senior season. The only good part was I had a car, so at least I didn't have to hang around for hours waiting on my mom to pick me up anymore.

During that fall semester, my mom finally let me live with my dad. She was out of touch with reality, and I was in the way of her lifestyle. She wanted to get high for days on end and then crash for as long as she needed. My dad had remarried by that time. His wife, Karen, was a very loud, opinionated person, but I liked her well enough, and my dad seemed to be happy. I was working, playing football, and going to school, so I stayed busy. I thought everything was fine. Then, after a few months, my dad kicked me out of the house. He said it was because I spilled food on my bedsheets one night while eating ribs, and Karen got so mad she gave him an ultimatum: either I had to leave or she would. He had fought for years to get custody of me, and it ended just like that. I couldn't grasp the reasoning. He chose Karen over me. I had to go back to live with my mom and her drug-addict friends. How bad was it at this point? She and her friends would sit around and shoot BB guns in the house; not at targets, just into the wall, as if that were normal behavior. Even other drug addicts hanging out at our house would tell me she was insane. Welcome home.

When my dad kicked me out, I was shook. It caught me completely off guard, and I couldn't understand the reasoning. I went to Grandpa Jones's house to try and digest what had happened. I was exhausted with my living arrangements. As I vented to Grandpa Jones in his living room, I began to crack. The more I talked, the more I couldn't hold back the tears. I sat in front of him, bawling my eyes out, asking, "Why? Why doesn't my dad want me?" I pleaded, "I'm a good kid! I get good grades. I play football. I work. I don't get in trouble. Why doesn't he want me? He fought for years to get me!" My grandfather could say nothing that would console me as I broke down in his living room. But it was nice to have someone who would at least listen to me and understood a bit of my pain.

After leaving my grandfather's house, I drove around trying to make sense of what had happened. The only thing I could come up with was that my parents were looking out for themselves and not me. That's when I truly realized no one was going to look out for me. My mom hadn't put me first for as long as I could remember, and my dad chose his newest wife over me. I could not end up like my parents. I needed to figure out what was best for my future. If I was going to make it out, it was solely on me.

A few years later, after my dad and Karen got divorced, I learned the reason Karen had given others for why they kicked me out, and it didn't involve spilling food in bed. Grandfather Hope told me what Karen had told him: she and my dad kicked me out because I had a threesome in the bathroom with two girls before school one morning. I wish I was that interesting!

Imagine needing to discuss this with your very religious

grandfather; it wasn't an easy conversation. What actually happened was Cassondra, my girlfriend of two and half years, came over with one of her friends before school one Friday morning. I normally shaved my legs on Fridays because we had our ankles taped on game day. For fun, they shaved my legs for me that Friday. I told Dad and Karen days in advance what we were planning to do. We left the bathroom door open the whole time, had some laughs, and then went to school. It was just good old wholesome fun.

I believe the real reason Karen asked my dad to kick me out was because I was cheating on Cassondra with Karen's son's ex-girlfriend. Karen had set up that relationship and kept asking me to break up with Cassondra. Finally, I told her I wasn't breaking up with Cassondra, and my relationship with her son's ex-girlfriend didn't matter to me. I was kicked out of the house not long after. I'm positive that my ending the relationship with her son's ex-girlfriend was the main motive for kicking me out.

Finally, the last game of the season arrived. Since it was senior night, I was allowed to start. At halftime, they were going to announce the seniors as our parents accompanied us onto the field. I told my mom what time to be there (actually, I told her it started earlier than it did to make sure she wasn't late). I told her to let me know if she couldn't make it so I could work out something else. I knew I could ask a grandparent, Noah, Grace, Dad, or someone else to be there for me. She insisted on coming and promised she would be there. When that night arrived, I lined up with my senior teammates near the center of the field, facing the line of parents, a blank space where my mother should have been. The announcer called out the names of my senior teammates and their parents, who then walked toward each other, joined hands, and waved to the crowd. As I stood waiting for my turn, I searched for Mom to appear, hopeful she would show up at the last minute. But she never did. When my and Mom's names were announced, I walked to the center of the field by myself. After a few seconds, my friend's mom walked over to accompany me so I wasn't standing in the middle of the field alone. Nothing was more important to me at that moment. I had fought so hard to get back to being able to play football through my injuries, and feeling like it meant nothing to anyone besides me was devastating. It may not sound like much, but that moment stuck with me. It was so embarrassing to be stood up by my own mom for all my teammates and the crowd to see.

I was back to going through the motions and struggling. One beacon of light that year was my Uncle Noah and Aunt Grace. They encouraged me to go to college. Actions speak louder than words, and their actions meant everything to me. I went to their home and ate dinner with them once a week. During that time, they helped me apply for college, student loans, and scholarships. I never really tried in school, and it showed in my essays for college scholarships. Grace helped me by proofreading them and giving me honest feedback about how bad the first drafts were. Uncle Noah had honest conversations with me about my subpar effort, which helped me grow and mature. They showed me a way out of what I thought was normal. I don't know if I could have achieved what I have without them, and I consider myself lucky to have had their support. I know I said it earlier, but having someone love you and believe in you is powerful.

COLONEL TENNIS TEAM: Members of the Henderson County boys tennis team are, front row from left, Trent Arn, Stephen Hope, Alex Gish and Chris Dunaway; second row, A.J. Hayes, Michael Chapman, Zack Gregory and coach Allen Hawkins. Not pictured are Mason Johnson, Andrew Swanson, Jonathan Newman, Isaac Duncan and Steven Jones. (Gleaner photo by Darrin Phegley • 831-8375 or dphegley@thegleaner.com)

After football season was over in the fall, I had no sports to keep me busy in the spring semester. I didn't want to spend any more time at home than I had to, so I joined the tennis team. Between bagging groceries, going to school, and playing tennis, the majority of my time was scheduled that semester. The only reason I went home was to sleep, and even sleeping there was difficult because of all the drug addicts going in and out of the house at every hour. Every chance I got, I stayed with friends. I stayed away from home at all costs. I even hated leaving my clothes there. I worked and, with the money I earned, I purchased a car, paid for insurance, and bought nice clothes for school. But my mom constantly borrowed my clothes and ruined them. She returned my shirts stretched out and wrinkled around the midsection from tucking them into her pants, with yellow stains all over them that wouldn't wash out. I later learned those were chemical stains from her drug use.

College couldn't come soon enough. Before I left for college, some friends and I went to a house party. As we got out of the car, Malik, one of my childhood bullies, greeted us. This was my first time seeing him since he used to beat me up after school. The minute he saw me, he started yelling, "Yo, I used to beat this guy's ass after school!" I was bigger now, so I told him, "Try it again." Then I repeated, "Try it again, now!" He sized me up and smiled. I said again, "I'm not a little kid anymore. Try it now."

I didn't really hold a grudge or anything against him, but since he was boasting about bullying me, I wanted him to prove he still could. Plus, I really don't like bullies. In all honesty, he probably could have mopped the floor with me, and as soon as his friends caught wind that he was fighting, they would have joined in to beat my ass. But I didn't care. It was all fun and games to him, but at that moment, I was ready if he wanted to test the waters.

While everyone else walked to the party, Malik and I stood on the sidewalk a bit longer. I said again, "I'm not a little kid anymore. Try it now." Then, he tossed his arm around me with a smile, we talked it out for a bit, and we joined the party. After that, I really liked him and later got to know and like some of his friends as well. I'm truly glad nothing violent happened that night. But you never know when those emotions from the past will get the best of you. The physical pain of getting my ass kicked would still have been better than sitting at the drug house I called home.

CHAPTER 7

FIRST YEAR OF COLLEGE

GETTING OUT

Me at Project Early Start.

I WAS ACCEPTED INTO WESTERN KENTUCKY UNIVERSITY. I received two small scholarships: one from the local bank, and one for participating in Project Early Start. The summer before college, I worked in a local factory to save money. That job wasn't too bad, and I worked only forty hours a week. The hardest part was not smoking weed long enough to pass the drug test before I started. I started smoking weed in ninth grade, and each year, I smoked more and more frequently. By my senior year, I was smoking weed a couple times a day and before most events, including family functions and work. It helped slow my mind down at the time.

Once I got to college, the one thing I promised myself was that I would never miss class. I knew that even if my grades were not great, it would help if I showed up and the teacher saw the effort I was putting in. I still wondered if I had the mental capacity to keep up with everyone else after my experiences in the special classes, so I thought showing up to every class could potentially give me the boost I needed to pass. Also, if the class had an attendance policy, I wouldn't ever have to worry.

My major was healthcare administration. I chose that field with the help of my aunt and uncle. I wanted to be a stockbroker like Noah, but he said it wouldn't be a good job in the future. They wanted me to pick a major that would allow me to always be able to find a job after graduation.

I did pretty well my first semester. I had a 3.14 GPA. I roomed with my best friend. Elrod and I were attached at the hip. We were basically brothers. We both played football and enjoyed hunting and fishing. We had spent tons of time together from grade school through high school. Hope and Elrod, or Elrod and Hope—we did almost everything together. About halfway through the first semester, I could tell he was struggling. I offered to help him study or with whatever he needed, but he chose a different path. College isn't for everyone, and I don't think it was right for him. He seemed overwhelmed. When he started to struggle, he focused on things that hurt him, like maintaining a "tough guy" persona. He went out more, drank more, fabricated more stories, and acted like he didn't care about any consequences.

One weekend, we took a trip to the University of Kentucky to hang out with some buddies. Elrod and I went outside to smoke a cigarette. We were both a little drunk and very high. I started rambling about something, and whatever I said set him off. He said, "Dude, you're freaking me out. You're being weird. Shut the fuck up." We jokingly said shit like this to each other all the time, but this time, it was different. He meant it, and at that moment, our relationship changed. That's when I knew Elrod and I were going down different paths. I was losing my best friend, who was like a brother to me. He was still around after that, but we drifted apart slowly until he finally left WKU after the first semester of our second year.

Late into my first semester, something began to change in my mind. Losing that tight, eight-year relationship with my best friend was hard. For almost as long as I could remember, we were always together. With him now absent, I spent more time alone with my thoughts. I wondered if something was wrong with me. My best friend no longer wanted to hang out with me, but I didn't feel I had changed in any way. I got quiet and spent too much time in my head, wondering if my reality was the same as everyone else's. When I went to class, I felt like everyone knew what I was thinking. I could hear them commenting about my thoughts, and then I'd feel bad about what they were "saying." It was extremely noisy and made it hard to pay attention in class. Imagine sitting at your desk while the teacher is talking and "hearing" everyone in the room heckle you about your innermost thoughts. It was hard to catch my breath at times and nearly impossible to hear the teacher over all the inner chatter. I knew what was happening couldn't be real, but I couldn't control it. It was maddening.

I think it was more than losing my best friend that caused my mind to go haywire. It was also a delayed reaction to the weight of being in college. Everything moved so fast when I first arrived at school—moving into the dorm, finding my classrooms, buying books, and just figuring out how everything operated—that I didn't have time to think or process what was happening. Once I got comfortable and slowed down, the enormity of the change in my life began to hit me. The financial burden was entirely on me; if I failed, there wasn't a backup plan. All these things, along with slowly losing my best friend and smoking too much weed in a fragile state, were taking a toll.

I had a public-speaking class that semester that terrified me. My stutter was better, but the fear of stuttering was always in the back of my mind. I was teaching myself how to study since I hadn't learned how in junior high or high school. I found what worked best for me was to find the quietest spot in the library with no distractions and go through the material over and over again. I used this approach to memorize a particular speech I had to give in my public-speaking class. I prepared as best I could, but being nervous really doesn't help a speech flow well no matter how much you practice ahead of time. I remember sitting in class with my heart in my mouth, sweating profusely while waiting my turn. After each person finished speaking, my anxiety increased, and the class got louder in my head. Breathing became difficult, and I considered walking out a few times. I wanted to stay because I had studied so hard, and I knew if I didn't give my speech that day, I'd just have to do it later.

The professor called my name, and I walked up to the

podium, notes in hand. I stumbled through my name and introduction, and then I dove into my speech. The speech only had to be five minutes long, but my hands were sweaty, and I ended up bending my note cards a little too much while fidgeting with them. They fluttered out of my grasp like a game of fifty-two-card pickup. I gave a little smile, and my heart sank back in my chest. I continued speaking while picking up the cards from the floor. I didn't miss a beat. The worst possible outcome had happened, yet that was the most comfortable speech I had ever given in that class. I realized all the anxiety and stress I had built up in my mind was my own creation. The speech felt like an impenetrable roadblock to overcome. In actuality, since I had prepared, I was able to breeze through it once I got out of my own way.

My second semester didn't go well. I think what I was going through mentally was taking a toll on my body. I developed an abscess on my back-right tonsil with three weeks of school left. I didn't want to go home for surgery until after I had finished the semester. I was extremely sick. It was like having strep throat for weeks with no relief. I would take my trash can with me to the dorm shower and flip it upside down. Then, I would sit on it for thirty minutes to two hours with hot water running over my body. I had to eat all soft foods, but it hurt to swallow anything, and I had no appetite. My grandma Cathy came down to check on me a few times and drop off some goodies, as most awesome grandmothers do. I still made it to most of my classes, but my weight dropped significantly, and I was exhausted.

The best thing during that time was that my mind slowed down. I had a goal of finishing the semester, and I felt too awful to worry about anything else. It sucked being sick, but when I was in class, I didn't have the crippling anxiety or voices flooding me. I got a D in a basic computer-literacy class that required a bunch of busy work, which I didn't have the capacity for, but I did okay in the rest of my classes that semester.

CHAPTER 8

BACK HOME FOR THE SUMMER

AS SOON AS I FINISHED THE SEMESTER AND RETURNED home for summer, I had surgery on my abscessed tonsil. Afterward, the doctor told me to take it easy because if I did too much strenuous activity, the abscess could open. But I was a young guy with things to do. Being young and dumb happens to all of us. I went out with friends the next day to watch the Henderson City Golf Tournament, where one of my friends was a few shots back of the lead. We rode around in golf carts, drinking and smoking for a few hours, and then planned to spend the rest of the day on a boat. All of this was against my doctor's orders, of course.

On the way to the river, I drank vodka and Tom Collins mix from a red Solo cup while smoking a cigarette. I suddenly felt my mouth fill with liquid. When I opened my mouth, blood filled the cup almost instantly. My friend Austin pulled over to the side of the road. I got out and opened my mouth, and blood flooded out; it was chunky, and the bleeding wouldn't stop. We decided to go to the hospital. I kept my cup with me in the car just in case it happened again, and it did, several times. About ten minutes into the drive, just after we passed the small airport in Geneva, Kentucky, everything went blurry. I told Austin, "I can't see. My vision is gone." Everything went blank. I thought I was done.

The next thing I knew, I was at the hospital, sitting in a room holding a plastic tub. Every so often, I opened my mouth, and blood continued to flow out. I didn't know the body could lose that much blood (it felt like over a gallon) and stay alive. The hospital had to call in an off-duty surgeon to cauterize the wound. The surgeon saw my name and told me Grandfather Hope had been his first patient when he started his practice! I thought that was pretty cool and a definite advantage of growing up in a small town. He also told me I had the biggest vein he had ever seen near the tonsil that was bleeding. It was a scary day, but I knew I needed to take it easy for a while after that to let it heal. That's what it took to keep me from doing dumb-kid stuff after surgery.

That summer, I worked at a different factory in Henderson, Kentucky, called Naad Corp. My friend Quinn's dad was the superintendent of the plant, and seven of my friends worked there too. My goal was to save up enough money to get through the next fall and spring semesters of college. That factory job was a lot different than what I'd experienced in past summers. I arrived before the sun came up and left when it was going down. We worked a minimum of twelve hours a day, seven days a week, and sometimes we worked fourteen-hour and sixteen-hour days. That's overtime, double-time, and triple-time. More money? Yes, please, I'll take it!

I smoked weed every morning on the way to work and then sometimes during break time and lunch. After my first month at the factory, I started driving a stand-up fork truck, building part orders to be delivered. Driving around stoned on one of those things was kind of fun. One day, I was moving some axles around and turned a corner a bit too quickly, accidentally dumping a full pallet of axles right in front of my supervisor. After any accident, drivers were supposed to be drug tested immediately. I got down and started loading the axles back onto the pallet. That's when my supervisor asked if I could pass a drug test. I looked at him and said, "No." Thank God I was honest because he didn't make me take one.

It was a brutal summer of nonstop work but I made around $13,000, which I thought was an insane amount of money. I made two big purchases before heading back to school. First, I bought a guitar, which was one of the worst purchases I ever made. I quickly lost interest in learning to play, so I sold it for extra money about a year later. Second, I bought a pound of weed for $800, which turned out to be a great investment. I sold it all in the first six months of my sophomore year, earning a profit of $1,200, even after smoking most of it myself. All my spare money the past three years had gone toward weed. Now, I was able to smoke as often as I wanted and turn a profit. I sold only to friends I smoked with, so I never had to be around sketchy people. It was a great little side hustle.

CHAPTER 9

SOPHOMORE YEAR OF COLLEGE

NOT WHAT I EXPECTED

MY SECOND YEAR OF COLLEGE WAS MY FIRST YEAR LIVING off campus. WKU requires students to live on campus the first two years, but executive committee members of fraternities are allowed to live in frat houses. I never imagined I'd join a frat, but I really wanted to live off campus. A bunch of kids from my hometown rushed Kappa Sigma, so I did too. Kappa Sig had just been reinstated at WKU and was on the rise. Being a part of something like that was very appealing to me. I wanted to belong to a team again. My high school football team had been my family, and I missed it. Being a part of building up a team or community sounded great. I became the treasurer so I could live at the frat house, and I got what I thought was the best room in the house. It had a big closet and a sink in the room. What more did I need?

That fall semester was one of the craziest periods of my life. First, Uncle Noah called and told me my mom had been arrested and was going to jail. She had sold meth from our home in Henderson, Kentucky, to an undercover cop. She had been cooking meth in the backyard shed, right there in her neighborhood of small, cookie-cutter homes that butted up to one another. I couldn't be a naive kid anymore. My mom was going to jail.

Her behavior when I was growing up finally started to make sense. She was a monster for all those years because of drugs. I thought back to all the hours I sat alone on sidewalks waiting for her to pick me up, her not being there on the fifty-yard line when they announced our names at senior night, beating my head against the wall trying to take care of Gunner without knowing how, getting yelled at during all those car rides because her family cared about her—all of it was because she chose drugs. She was too busy doing drugs, or passed out recovering from doing drugs, to be a mom.

But my strongest reaction to the news of my mom's arrest was concern for Gunner. She still took him to her house one night a week and every other weekend. I was already frustrated with her because she allowed Gunner to hang out with some bad kids that lived down the street. One time, they sent Gunner over a fence into a kennel containing two pit bulls, and those dogs tore my little brother apart. The other kids finally saved him by tossing meat from their refrigerator into the kennel to keep the dogs occupied while they pulled Gunner to safety. He had to have plastic surgery to put his face back together. Gunner should never have been around those kids, but anyone under my mom's supervision had no supervision. I'm sure when it happened she was either passed out or locked in the bathroom picking at the "monster in the mirror" like she had been for most of my childhood. (Heavy meth users often stare into the mirror for hours, picking at the meth-induced sores on their faces.)

Allowing Gunner around those kids was one thing, but taking him from a safe place to a meth lab? Putting him, unsupervised, into an environment with dangerous chemicals that could blow up at any time? That was unacceptable. I was used to her treatment of me. I was damaged, and suffering the brunt of her actions felt normal. But seeing her neglect someone besides me, my own little brother, was too much. She gave birth to me, but any chance of a meaningful relationship between us vanished that day.

After digesting the news, I made a second promise to myself: I would never be dependent on a substance. My mother's substance abuse ruined her life and nearly caused me to end mine. I have to deal with emotional scars for the rest of my life because of her substance abuse. I know addiction is an awful thing and it consumes the addict, but it also molds the people who grow up in the addict's world. One of my recurring nightmares from childhood perfectly sums up the experience of being raised by an addict. The dream always started out positive, with me playing with friends. Then, dark clouds with menacing facial expressions would come rolling in, wreaking havoc. My friends would disappear. All the light would be shadowed out as the massive storm clouds blew everything around. All the goodness and joy from my surroundings would disappear. I would be shaking and scared in the dream, curled into a ball, while the storm clouds broke loose on me with all their might. I always woke from this dream terrified, screaming and crying. The way I felt in the dream was how I felt every day growing up with this addict I called Mom.

I wish what happened next during that hellish semester had been a dream. I went back to Henderson for the wedding of two great high school friends, Lauren and Kyle. Lauren was one of the friends who used to let me sleep at her house when I wanted to avoid my own. The wedding was fun. I remember eating plenty of the three different kinds of cake they served, and I got to catch up with a bunch of hometown friends I hadn't seen in years. At one point, I was outside smoking a cigarette when the cops showed up and told everyone to leave the parking lot and go inside. They threatened to start arresting people. I was by the door, but Elrod was in the parking lot, so I walked over to tell him the cops were ushering us inside. We headed to the door, but a police officer stopped us. I explained we were on our way back to the wedding and I had gone to the parking lot to get my friend when the other officer told us everyone needed to go inside.

The cop asked for our IDs and told us to wait there. When he came back, he told me to come with him. He walked me around to the back of the venue and told me to go inside. I said I didn't want to. He said someone was causing trouble in the back bar of the venue. I didn't even know that bar existed. I explained I was at a wedding all night and had nothing to do with anything that happened at the bar. Still, the cop put me in handcuffs and forced me inside.

Once inside, he asked the bartender if it was me who had been causing trouble, and the bartender said no. The cop took me, still handcuffed, to the wedding reception area and paraded me down the aisle and out the front door in front of Lauren's and Kyle's families and all my friends. I kept asking what was going on and telling the cop I hadn't done anything. Once I was out front, the officer made me wait in front of the venue in handcuffs for everyone to see. Then he came back, uncuffed me, gave me my ID, and walked off without a word—no apology, nothing. This was one of the most humiliating moments of my life, and I felt bad for Lauren and Kyle, who had to have been embarrassed for all this happening in front of their families. I still don't know if they were just making an example of me to try to keep everyone at the venue in line or if, since my mom was a known meth user/dealer, they wanted to find something on me. Either way, the memory still haunts me. As does what happened that holiday season.

The next incident of that semester also happened in Henderson, when I went home for Christmas break. I spent the majority of my time with my friend Roger and his family. I also bounced between both sides of my family, the Hopes and the Joneses. Some friends and I went out to a local bar downtown to catch up with other old friends. Kyle and Lauren were sitting at the bar with Kyle's dad and mom when we arrived. I had spent a lot of time at Kyle's house growing up and had been around his mom, dad, and sister plenty, so I waved at them. Instead of waving back, Kyle's dad, a churchgoing fellow, gave me the most disgusted look I've ever received in my life. That look made me feel like I was one inch tall. I was delighted when I got to talk with Lauren and Kyle before they left, but man, that look—I'll never forget it. I understood where Kyle's dad was coming from. I was the kid whose mom was in jail for operating a meth lab in her backyard and the kid who embarrassed him in front of his family by being paraded down the middle of his son's wedding in handcuffs. Wearing the burden of my mom's meth addiction.

Back at school, I was taking an anatomy and physiology class, which included a lab. I studied for that lab more than I had for any other class in my life. The class was easy, but the lab was brutal. I actually sold weed to one of the lab teachers, but it didn't help. I failed the lab, which meant I failed the class. So, I would have to retake both the class and the lab the following fall. Most students had to retake this class two or three times before they passed, but failing was still a gut punch after putting in all those hours of studying.

On top of that, I had issues with my ex-girlfriend Cassondra, who had recently started going to WKU as well. We had dated all four years of high school and into my first semester of college, but I was an idiot and cheated on her. After just one week of dating, I was drinking at a friend's house and got a little too drunk. The next thing I knew, a hot girl was on top of me, kissing me. I didn't stop her, and I should have. We ended up going back to her friend's place, where she wanted to do more, but I was too drunk. Even so, that's not how you start a relationship.

I continued to do stuff like that the entire time we dated. Constantly cheating on Cassondra made me a bad and extremely jealous boyfriend. What I put her through was ridiculous. The worst was when I had a two-night fling with a girl I met at a party, caught an STD, and passed it on to Cassondra. She found out at a medical checkup. I didn't have any symptoms, but I got a checkup and found out I had it too. Thank goodness it wasn't a bad STD. I had to drink some chalky stuff, take some pills, and it was gone. I also had to tell the other girl who I was hanging out with at the time. After that, I did the worst thing I have ever done in my dating life. I blamed the STD on Cassondra, my girlfriend of four years. I denied, denied, denied, just like I had during our whole relationship. I feel terrible about the way I treated her. She didn't deserve it. That incident was the nail in the coffin of our relationship and sealed the deal on us breaking up.

Even so, Cassondra and I talked every now and then since we were both at WKU. Sometimes, we'd hang out, and eventually, all those feelings came rushing back for me. In my mind, I wanted to make it right. I decided to go all in, if she would have me. I bought a calendar and wrote "I still love you" on each page. That night, I met her near the fine-arts building in a concrete outdoor stadium. I confessed my love for her and promised to never repeat my same mistakes again. I was ready to devote my life to her forever, no matter what. She turned down my offer, which, looking back, was obviously the right thing to do. Who could blame her for rejecting the cheesy gibberish coming from an asshole like me? An asshole who was lost and desperate.

The semester wasn't over yet. I took Quinn with me to one of our frat parties, where he met a beautiful, young lady. She was fun and had a great personality, and they ended up dating for quite a while. We all got along well. One night a week, we made dinner together, smoked some weed, and watched movies. It was great. One rainy night, we had planned to eat spaghetti, but Quinn's girlfriend didn't show up. Quinn tried to call her a few times, but she didn't answer. Eventually, one of her friends got in touch with Quinn and told us she had been in a car accident not even a block from my frat house. We headed straight to the ER. The police and hospital staff would not tell us anything. We spent the whole night at the hospital waiting to learn how she was doing and keeping her parents updated on what was going on. It felt like an eternity. The entire time, Quinn kept breaking down over the possibilities of what might be wrong. I felt helpless. There was nothing I could do or say to make it better. The only thing I could do at that moment was be there for him. When Quinn's phone died, his girlfriend's parents began calling me instead of Quinn for updates, but I had no information from the hospital or authorities. After talking with the parents and feeling their desperation, I couldn't keep it together either. Something bad had happened to their little girl, and there was nothing anyone could do.

It wasn't until the next morning that we learned she had

died on impact in the accident. We waited all fucking night for them to tell us this information. They knew she was dead at the scene, but they strung us along for countless hours, letting her parents and friends sit in uncertainty, bawling their eyes out as they worried. Something was fishy about the whole thing. Later, I learned an off-duty police officer was driving, late for work, when he hit her. The police and local news buttoned up the situation to make it look pretty, changing the story two or three times before it was put to rest, but I had a hard time believing it. My frat brothers and I knew firsthand that cop cars often sped down Kentucky Street to get to their headquarters about a mile away, as if the law didn't apply to them. We frequently saw them driving over fifty miles per hour on this small, local street with a speed limit of thirty-five. The location where she was hit is extremely dangerous, especially when cars are speeding. Suspecting there was a cover-up made losing a wonderful person even harder. Her family reached a $1 million settlement with the city of Bowling Green six years later. The story was also different in that report. We lost such a great, kind, and gentle person. I know I and so many others will never forget her.

That semester of college was definitely the semester from hell. I failed my first class; my mom went to jail for making and selling meth; I couldn't right a wrong with my high school sweetheart; I was publicly embarrassed by cops in my hometown; I was publicly snubbed by a friend's father, whom I respected; and I lost a sweet and kind friend under suspicious circumstances. My only option was to keep moving forward, but how? I was caught in a stagnant cycle of being lost and going through the motions. I was desperate to not end up back home. I had to make changes.

One big change I decided to make was to stop smoking weed so much. It was hurting me mentally and physically. Every time

I smoked, I felt crippling anxiety and experienced physical pain in my nasal cavities, as if they were being pulled apart. Also, everything around me appeared animated, which might sound cool but was actually scary. I didn't completely stop, but I drastically reduced my usage. Instead of smoking daily, I smoked only once every month or two, if that.

* * *

All of the turmoil in the fall led to me questioning my choice of major in the spring. I had chosen healthcare administration for the stability it would provide me—for the girlfriend I no longer had and the future family I had planned. With all of that gone, sticking with healthcare administration didn't seem as important. I wasn't enjoying my classes. Plus, I had failed a class. It was time to choose a major for myself, not others. I asked myself, *What do you enjoy doing?* I loved playing golf. *What careers involve golf?* I could work in a golf pro shop as a head pro or outside maintaining a golf course. I liked being outside, so I leaned toward golf-course maintenance. I asked Quinn a bunch of questions about it since that was his major, and then I worked with my WKU advisor to make the leap from healthcare administration to my new major: horticulture with an emphasis in turfgrass. It was a hard decision, but I was ready for the change. I tried to get a summer internship at a nice club in the area, but it was too late in the game for that summer; they were full. I still wanted experience working in golf-course maintenance, so I applied for and got an hourly position at a local municipal golf course.

CHAPTER 10

SUMMER INTERNSHIPS

WORKING AT THE MUNICIPAL GOLF COURSE WAS A LEARN-ing experience for me. I might have been the worst employee they ever had. I lacked experience and had a habit of showing up late or not at all. My boss was an absolute saint not to fire me because he had every reason to.

Drinking and driving was much more common back then. For fun in high school, we'd get a bunch of beer or whiskey and either go bow fishing or, if the backwater wasn't up, drive around in the river bottoms and shoot guns. That's life in a small town. One night that summer, my frat brothers and I were shoveling a big pile of sand in the backyard of the frat house to create a sand volleyball court, all the while drinking the frat house dry of alcohol. Once the sand was shoveled into place, we played volleyball late into the night and next morning. I had to go to work at the course in about four hours, so I headed home. I rolled through a stop sign about a block from my house, not noticing the cop nearby. I pulled into my driveway and was almost to the door when the cop shined a light on me and ordered me to stop.

I failed the sobriety test miserably, blowing a 0.23. The legal limit was 0.08. I was going to jail. I could not hide it from my boss when I showed up extremely late the next day, after I got out of jail. I felt like a huge failure at the time, but that's what it took for me to stop drinking and driving. I had to go to DUI classes every week and pay some hefty fines. I was broke, so paying the fines was backbreaking. I wasn't allowed to drive, but a coworker I had become friends with volunteered to give me rides to and from work until I got my hardship license. Miraculously, my boss still didn't fire me.

Despite my subpar performance as an employee, that summer on the golf course was a great learning experience. I learned how to change cups, perform course setup, rake bunkers, and mow greens, fairways, and rough. I also did a lot of weed eating. The most important thing I learned was how much maintenance crews depend on one another to complete each daily task. Most maintenance crews don't have an unlimited labor force, and so one asshole (me) taking the day off without informing the supervisor throws a monkey wrench into everything and makes things harder for everyone. My boss, Tony, explained this to me. It may not have clicked at the time, but those conversations we had will stick with me forever. He didn't have to have those real conversations with me. I was there for only a summer, and he would likely never see me again. He took time out of his day to try and help me, and that helped the team. He's truly one of the good ones and still working at that golf course in Bowling Green, Kentucky.

✻ ✻ ✻

Despite the lessons I learned that summer, I still wondered if I had made the right decision in changing my career path. I ignored my doubts and continued to move forward. During my junior year of college, I applied again for the summer internship at River Rock, the nice course in town. This time I got it, so that's what I did the summer after my junior year.

My job at River Rock consisted of hand-watering fairways, walk-mowing approaches, and fly-mowing bunker banks. I also got to mow fairways and greens, top-dress tees with sand, and do routine things on a golf course that I had never done before. The worst job out there was fly-mowing: using a little mower that hovers a few inches above the ground to cut grass on steep slopes, like bunkers or lake banks. Eight of us would go out at 6:00 a.m. and fly-mow all day until about 5:30 p.m. It was a long day and hard work. My back was on fire the whole time. It still hurt from my football injury, and fly-mowing really got it going. I wore my regular work boots on my first day of fly-mowing, and I kept falling on the steep slopes that were nearly straight up and down. I couldn't do anything about my back, but I could do something to stop from falling. I brought in an old pair of football cleats to fly-mow in, so at least I didn't fall as much.

Even though the job was difficult at times, the experience was great, if for nothing else than to simply get reps in on all the different golf course tasks. The internship was very different from my municipal course job the previous summer. River Rock had all new equipment, two huge maintenance shops, and about twenty-five employees. Two other guys from my school interned with me. No doubt about it, I had the least experience of anyone, and this boss was much less forgiving than Tony had been.

At the end of the summer, I asked my boss if I could use some of the course's fertilizer for a class project in which I had to grow a particular turfgrass from seed and give a presentation on it. He gave me a fertilizer with dimension in it. I didn't know what that was, but I trusted he wouldn't steer me wrong. Well, I learned that dimension is a preemergent that stops seeds from growing. So, my seeds never grew, and I had to redo the project. That may not sound like much, but it left a bad taste in my mouth regarding my boss. When you're a struggling college student paying for everything yourself, any setback hurts—especially when it's caused by someone you are supposed to be leaning on for knowledge and support.

I was still paying DUI fines that summer, and I fell behind on my payments. One day at work, the police showed up and took me back to jail. It was embarrassing and not a great look for me or the course. But with my next paycheck, I was able to get caught up and out of jail.

I was still learning what it took to work on a golf course. It's not as easy as it might look. The hours are brutal, and the pay is low. I was thankful my boss let me work well into the fall semester, until he let the majority of the crew go before winter. I needed a job at all times. I had not made nearly as much money on golf courses as I had from my previous factory job, and I was not able to save any money. Between paying DUI fines and the cost of living, I kept little to no money in my bank account, but I was able to scrape by.

❦ ❦ ❦

Going into my fourth year of college, I was still questioning whether I had made the right decision by switching my major. Completing all my classes for the new major was going to take an extra semester plus a J-term (a minisemester during winter break) because one of the classes I needed to graduate was only available in the J-term. Also, I had to have two internships to graduate. I had one set up for the following summer, but the closer it got, the more my internship contact reduced the pay and benefits. So, I started looking elsewhere. The only good superintendent I'd heard of was Jason Cobb, the person who built River Rock, the course where I had just interned, and the current superintendent at Bear Din Golf Club in the suburbs of Chicago.

I was in a small-engines class that year with a guy who had interned with Jason the summer before. I was sitting next to this classmate when Jason called to ask if he knew anyone interested in interning for him the next summer. I figured this was my opportunity. I had heard stories from his past employees and sales reps about how innovative he was in the turf profession, so I called Jason as soon as class got out and locked up the internship. I also had a quick meeting with him at that year's golf-course industry show in Orlando, Florida. Everything went well, so I planned to go to Chicago for the summer.

The internship ended up being split between two courses. I spent the first half of the summer working with Jason at Bear Din Golf Club and the second half working with Brian Simpson at the Standard Club. One thing I've always done is work my ass off. I always believed I lacked intelligence, so I needed to make up for it in my work capacity. I believe I did a good job of showing this at both these internships.

After working with Jason, I finally knew changing my career path to golf-course maintenance was the right choice. His energy and passion for his profession were intoxicating. He showed me how to have fun with the job and that it's okay to do so. I worked my ass off for him, and he invited me back to be the second assistant at Bear Din the next April, after I graduated. The position was going to pay around $35,000 per year. I was sold. All I had to do was graduate on time and I would have my first job after college all lined up.

When I moved to the Standard Club, I learned Brian and Jason did things completely differently, but each style worked at its course. Brian was an established superintendent; he had spent sixteen years as the assistant at the Standard Club before taking over as superintendent. He already had his course dialed in with what he was trying to accomplish. I earned $1.50 per hour more at the Standard Club than at Bear Din, but my net income ended up being the same at both places because I worked fewer hours on a consistent schedule at the Standard Club. While Bear Din had a bunch of projects going at all times because we were trying to get the course back up to par after previous superintendents had let it go a little, the Standard Club was already top-notch. It was the most well-built and thought-out course I've seen from a maintenance perspective. The dual internship allowed me to work at two great places for industry-leading superintendents. By the end of the summer, I was ready to finish my classes, graduate, and start working with a renewed passion for my major.

CHAPTER 11

LAST YEAR OF COLLEGE

THE HOME STRETCH

IN ORDER TO GRADUATE AND START MY NEW JOB IN CHI-cago on time, I had to address two major concerns. The first was figuring out how to take the J-term class I needed. The problem was it cost money to take the class, and I was tapped out. It's not that I wasn't earning money; I was working twenty to thirty hours a week as a server at Logan's Roadhouse plus had a full class load at WKU. But I couldn't pay an up-front $2,500 for the J-term on top of paying for rent, utilities, and food. I tried getting financial aid but couldn't. A recurring theme with financial aid was that my dad limited its availability because he had a job. I always tried to pretend I didn't know him nor had a relationship with him to get more financial aid, but proving that is nearly impossible, so it didn't work. My dad didn't or couldn't help me pay for college, and that was fine. I didn't expect anyone's help.

However, I needed financial help to pay for the J-term.

Grandfather Hope was the man I asked. I explained I wouldn't have enough money in time to enroll in the J-term, but I promised I would pay the money back in the spring once I was able to get caught up financially. He gladly gave me the $2,500 with a smile. Grandmother Hope was more on the fence about it. I don't think she thought I would pay it back.

I passed the J-term with no problem, and I paid back my grandparents in April. My grandfather's smile was much bigger when I followed through on my word to pay him back. I could tell he was proud, and that felt amazing. He was the family member I felt understood me best. I think it was because our personalities were similar. He trusted me and knew I was trying to better myself.

When not working on a golf course, I was a server at the local Logan's Roadhouse. I was scared shitless when I started there because I had to talk in front of people, but it ended up becoming something I really enjoyed and was by far one of the best jobs I've ever had. After I had worked there only six months, I was moved to the opening and closing shifts and assigned the best sections. I had come a long way from my irresponsibility at my first municipal golf-course job and learned that having a strong work ethic helps in every profession.

The second major concern in my final semester was that I had to take an advanced Spanish class. Because I took two Spanish classes in high school, I couldn't take a basic or beginner course to fulfill my college foreign-language requirement. But it had been four years since I last took high school Spanish, and back then, I just memorized everything for the tests or cheated, so I basically didn't learn anything. Therefore, I really struggled in college-level Spanish. My professor mainly spoke in Spanish, and everything went over my head. The only thing I could do was show up for class every day and show the teacher I was trying. If I had to do it again, I would take a different foreign language so I could enroll in a basic class.

Whether or not I passed Spanish came down to the final. I had to get above an eighty-seven to pass the course. I thought, *There's no chance in hell I can pass that final, let alone earn a grade above an eighty-seven.* I decided the only way to pass, and therefore be able to graduate, was to cheat. We had to take the final under the professor's supervision in the computer lab, where she would give us the exam login information right before the test began. A girl I had dated on and off during college was excellent at Spanish and had passed the course the previous year, so I set her up at my apartment on my desktop. The plan was that once I received the login, I would text it to her. I would act like I was working until she finished the test. Then, once she had submitted her version of the final, I'd get up and leave. Turns out, I texted her the wrong information. I forgot to capitalize one letter of the login credentials, so she couldn't access the test. I was on my own. I was the last one to finish and knew I had failed. It was a hard pill to swallow. It meant I couldn't graduate in time to start at Bear Din in April.

Before I left the computer lab, I talked with the professor. I explained I had a job lined up for after graduation, and this was the only class keeping me from graduating. I had come to every class, sat in the front, and made an effort every day. I also explained I tried everything to get into a lower-level Spanish class because I was not ready for this class. She said I should've talked with her earlier, but she did seem to understand the situation. When I left, I knew I'd failed the final miserably, but I held a glimmer of hope she might pass me anyway. I waited on pins and needles until she posted my final grade. To my surprise, she passed me with a D.

That professor was a saint, and I can't thank her enough for helping me continue to move forward. With her understanding and help, I did it. I knew I would graduate in time to start my life in the real world. I still had a J-term class to pass in world regional geography that winter, but I didn't foresee any issues.

CHAPTER 12

BEAR DIN

LIFE IS GOOD

I GRADUATED AFTER PASSING MY J-TERM CLASS THAT winter, but my job as a second assistant for Jason at Bear Din Golf Club didn't start until April. So, I picked up as many shifts as possible at Logan's Roadhouse until it was time to head north to Chicago. Unfortunately, I blew the majority of my money on a trip to Florida right before I made the move. The only positive takeaway from that trip was I decided to stop smoking cigarettes on the way back. I always told myself I would quit after college. It was a habit I had picked up in high school. Before quitting, I was smoking nearly a pack a day.

I had only talked with the guys at Bear Din a few times since Jason offered me the job the previous summer. Right before my move, I was informed I would no longer be the second assistant. Instead, Jason was making me and one of the guys I interned with assistants in training (AITs). The new job paid twelve dollars an hour—a lot less than the $35,000-per-year salary originally offered. This was a big blow to the gut, but I was committed and determined to keep moving forward.

I stayed with Uncle Noah the night before I left for Chicago. When he found out I had blown the majority of my money, he let me have it. The lecture was because he cared, and I was a young knucklehead who needed to be lectured. Even though he was mad, he lent me some cash to help before I got my first paycheck. Aunt Grace did a budget exercise with me to show how I was going to pay it back in monthly payments. These were the life lessons I needed, and I'm thankful they both cared about me so much. My uncle had also given me his minivan the previous year, replacing my Pontiac Grand Am that had 275,000 miles and worked on its own timeline. You didn't tell the Grand Am when to start; she told you when and if she would start. So getting the minivan was huge! You never appreciate having a reliable car until you don't have one.

I arrived at my new job without incident. The other AIT, Jack Mabe, and I rented a condo together in downtown Arlington Heights. It was the nicest place I had ever lived. Student loans were going to start in a few months, and the struggle was going to be real. At the end of our first week, we all went out in downtown Chicago to celebrate. I remember walking back to our place from the train station and feeling a sense of calm rush over me. I knew I had made the right choice, and everything was going to work out.

The hours and workload at Bear Din were insane, but I was learning from some of the best in the business. My goal was to be like a sponge and absorb all the information I could from this opportunity. You never know what's going to happen next, and I needed to be prepared. There was a buzz of infectious enthusiasm in the maintenance department. I had always been a strong worker but was now learning how to use that energy to improve the course. We did all the normal maintenance expected of a top private club in Chicago plus we installed an irrigation system while also renovating as many greenside bunkers as possible in-house. Breaking up the mundane maintenance with these exciting projects helped me focus on all tasks.

We were getting toward the end of the season when Jason accepted a job at Colt Golf Club, one of the most exclusive clubs in Chicago—maybe *the* most exclusive. This threw me for a loop. I expected him to ask me to go with him before he left, but that conversation never happened. The only person on our staff he took with him was our mechanic, Scott. I talked with Scott before he left and told him I wanted to go with Jason. He explained Jason didn't want to leave Bear Din in a bad position by stealing a lot of people. He suggested I call Jason and maybe go see him. That's exactly what I did. I told Jason I had moved to Chicago to work for him, not Bear Din Golf Club. He outlined everything he had planned for his new course and invited me on board as his first assistant.

CHAPTER 13

COLT

THE FALLING OUT

IT WAS ALMOST WINTER WHEN I MADE THE MOVE TO COLT
Golf Club, but the grounds staff was still going a million
miles per hour improving the course. As first assistant, I was
responsible for running the crew—scheduling, training, hiring,
disciplining, and more. My first issue was trying to manage an
older staff who had been doing the same things for thirty years.
They had learned a bunch of bad habits that were hard to break.
I was reshaping bunkers with a large crew when one of the guys
told me, "We don't get paid enough; that's why we don't work
hard. Our old boss knew this and didn't mind." Changing the
culture with this crew was going to be tough. My lack of leadership experience made it even harder.

The hours we were asked to work weeded out the majority of
the bad eggs who were just there to collect a paycheck. I never
wanted anyone to lose his job, but we also needed team members who were ready to help rather than fight the improvements

we had planned for the course. The crew was not used to being held accountable for their work quality. The person who ran the crew before me let the crew choose what jobs they wanted, and as long as they were out and looked busy, it was okay. The course's condition reflected that; it resembled a local, nine-hole municipal course that had been rumored to be shutting down for the past ten years but always remained open for another year.

Colt is a special place. You can feel its history as soon as you step into the club. Jason's vision for the golf course was to restore it close to its original design. One way Jason made an immediate impact was by rethinking all the course accessories. He found several old photos of the original paddleball washers and had replicas specially made. We made tee markers in-house out of cherry trees I removed from the course. Grandfather Jones did a lot of woodworking and branded his name on the bottom of each piece he made, so I suggested to Jason we brand the Colt logo into the new tee markers. He loved the idea. He changed everything on the course—the flags, flag sticks, benches, and trash cans—all of it improved. We reclaimed an unbelievable amount of fescue areas that had been let go for years, redefined greens and fairways, and added shortgrass walkways from greens to tees. That's how you make waves and create a buzz at a new job. Once we got the crew organized and on the same page, which took about eight months, we inspired other departments at the club. They saw the passion and positive changes happening and felt the buzz. It was infectious, and everyone was riding that wave.

I was learning so much about the job each and every day. A lot of tasks I was doing for the first time, but I always gave 110 percent. Toward the end of that summer, Jason said I could have a long weekend, which was amazing because I worked seven days a week. I was still making only twelve dollars an hour, but that year I made $36,000 because of the number of hours I worked.

During my time off, I planned to visit friends on the way back to my hometown of Henderson, where I would see family and friends and play golf. My first stop was in Louisville. I met up with my cousin Drew, and we had a fun day wakeboarding. I slammed my head hard on the water a few times, but I didn't think much of it. Afterward, I went to a friend's house and drank all night. The next day, my friends and I went wakeboarding again. My balance had been a bit off all day, but it was a blast being out in the boat with friends. I decided to do one last run on the wakeboard before I was done. When I jumped the wake, I slammed my head on the water again. It didn't feel like I slammed it that hard, but I immediately felt nauseous and had a pounding headache. I felt like I had another concussion.

I signaled to my friends that I was done wakeboarding, and I got my feet out of the bindings. It sucked; everyone was having so much fun. I reasoned that telling them I had a concussion would ruin the day for everyone. I decided to act like nothing happened. We stayed out cruising around, having fun, and no one noticed I was in pain. When we got back to the dock and pulled the boat out of the water, I pulled Drew aside. I explained what happened and why I hadn't said anything earlier. He didn't believe me, but at least someone else knew, in case something bad happened. I got back to my friend's house and took it easy for the night, consuming only a few more beers. I knew I couldn't go to sleep for a while with a head injury. My balance was off, I felt nauseous, I had a headache, my vision was a little blurry, and light and noise intensified everything. But finally, I fell asleep.

Once I woke up, I figured everything would be fine. But nope, I still had the nausea and headache. I continued driving to Henderson as planned. I was fighting off the pain pretty well. I even played golf. I played horribly but got through it by drinking the whole time. My balance was still off, and the pain intensified with noise and sunlight. I figured the pain and nausea had to go away at some point. I thought, *It's just a concussion.* We didn't understand concussions and brain injuries back then like we do today. A concussion was just something that happened. You shook it off and kept moving. I'd had plenty of concussions that were fine in a day or two. But this one was persistent.

I headed back to Chicago determined to work through the pain. With each task at work, my symptoms got worse. I wasn't getting any better. One night, after two weeks of suffering, I went out to eat with Jason, his dad, and a couple other people. My head was killing me, and I was still nauseous. I told Jason's dad that I might head to the emergency room after we finished eating.

The pain finally won that night, and I went to the emergency room. They did a CT scan. The next thing I knew, I was in a neck brace on a stretcher with an IV in my arm. They found bleeding on the right side of my brain. *Great,* I thought, *another brain injury.* The hospital first tried morphine for the pain, but it didn't work. Then they gave me Demerol, a synthetic morphine. That did the trick. When it began pumping through me, for the first time in three weeks, I was pain free. Having that IV was the greatest feeling. It was the only thing that took the pain away.

After a few days, I was discharged but told not to go back to work for four to six weeks. Because of my carelessness while wakeboarding, Jason was short one lead assistant for possibly six weeks during his first full season at his dream job. I was worried he would fire me if I told him the truth. I made up a story about banging my head against the rear passenger side window during a car accident with my cousin Drew. I know now I really screwed up. It was stupid to lie. You should always be honest, especially with your boss. My lies put a strain on our relationship that took years to repair.

Caring for myself while recovering was going to be hard. My mom was still in jail, so I contacted Grandfather Jones and his wife, Greta, whom we grandkids called Nanny. They offered to come get me and take me back to their house to stay until I recovered. I resisted at first because I hated leaving my job when I knew Jason needed me, but I wasn't in any condition to be an asset to Jason, so I agreed. I stayed with them as planned the first night or two. Then Uncle Noah suggested I come stay with them for a couple nights. I tried, but the house was so full of bright lights and kids and loud noises that my symptoms got worse, and I had to go back to the hospital. After giving me another CT scan, the hospital pumped me full of morphine again. I still had a significant amount of swelling, and there was blood on the right side of my brain. I heard the nurse say to my uncle, "Don't worry about Stephen right now. We gave him morphine. He can't feel a thing."

I spoke up, "I'm sorry, but I'm in just as much pain as I was when I walked in here. Whatever you gave me has not done anything." That prompted them to give me synthetic morphine again, and then I was pain free. They kept me in the hospital for another day or two, during which time I continued to ask for the synthetic morphine. It didn't last that long, and I wanted every second I could get of being pain free. I was still nauseous, so they gave me something for that as well.

When I was discharged from the hospital this time, I felt a lot better about my situation. The doctors laid out a plan for my recovery and sent me home with a steroid pack along with something for the nausea and pain. I just had to keep myself from being a dumbass long enough for my brain to recover. I went back to my grandparents' house and took it easy for the next several weeks. Even looking at my phone during this time caused my symptoms to get worse.

Doctors say different concussions aren't related to each other, but I don't know how that played out in my case. I think my first concussion made me prone to getting more. I believe when I banged my head and felt a little woozy that first day of wakeboarding, I had a minor concussion. Then, because I drank that night and wakeboarded again the next day before I was fully recovered, when I hit my head again, it opened up the floodgates for a brain injury. And who knows if I would have gotten a concussion either day if my helmet hadn't broken all those years ago?

It took the full six weeks before I felt like I could potentially go back to work. So, I headed back to Chicago. My relationship with Jason had obviously changed. He felt like I cheated him by taking so much time off, and he let me know it. He believed I owed him something I couldn't repay. My work was suffering. I was still not fully recovered, and the harder I tried, the worse my headaches got. Bouncing around on a golf course in full sun for the majority of each day was taking a toll on me. Worse still was the way I was getting called out by Jason. He said some hurtful things, like calling me dumb and stupid. He didn't know I already thought this of myself, and hearing it from him pushed me into an even worse headspace. It felt unfair that he kept harassing me despite all I had invested in him and my career. I thought there was no way he was going to help me get a superintendent job now. I was having negative thought after negative thought, and thinking positively about anything seemed impossible. The stress of the situation manifested into other physical ailments. I got ulcers. I couldn't sustain my work capacity anymore, the one thing I could always lean on. My mental state was drifting further into the darkness.

CHAPTER 14

GETTING BACK ON TRACK

HEROES APPEAR IN YOUR LIFE EVERY NOW AND THEN. JUST as Uncle Noah and Aunt Grace had come to my rescue to help me get into college, our mechanic, Scott Duckworth, helped me during this dark time in my life. When Jason went off on me, Scott stepped in to defend me. He told Jason I was struggling and my brain injury was to blame for my lack of performance, not who I was as a person. He told Jason, "You can't keep kicking this man while he's down. He's struggling and hasn't fully recovered." I know there are bad people out there, but there are also saviors. Scott didn't owe me anything, and I can never thank him enough for helping me get through this period.

My weight ballooned back up after the injury. Normally, the physical demands of my job would counteract whatever I ate that day. But, we were going into winter, where I would only work forty-four hours a week. Eating whatever I wanted without as much physical activity from my job wasn't working. I needed to get control of my weight and ever-worsening chronic back pain. I opted to do P90X, a set of high-intensity

DVD workouts done over the course of ninety days. I needed the consistent routine and meal guide the program offered. I had drifted into a bad mental state—the noise in my head had gotten louder, increasing my anxiety, and I'd started feeling more alone and depressed.

This stint in the darkness was a little worse than usual. I had not been active in the months I spent with my grandparents recovering from my brain injury. Plus, every day Nanny cooked some of the best food I had ever eaten while I was inactive and healing. I needed to get back on the right track. My headaches were still constant but more tolerable, but the thought of trying to work out worried me. I didn't want to strain too hard and cause the bleeding to restart. If that happened, my performance at work would suffer again, and who knew if I would get fired or not this time? I had student loans and a car payment; I couldn't afford to get fired. Not knowing how my body would react to working out was unnerving, but having dealt with a previous brain injury helped ease my fears. I just needed to listen to my body.

It took me a long time to pull the trigger and actually put the P90X plan into motion. I was in a bad headspace. My relationship with Jason was horrid, I couldn't keep up at work, I was fat again, I had constant migraines from my brain injury, and my chronic back pain was getting worse, limiting my work performance. The longer I let my negativity and health snowball, the deeper a hole I was digging, which was only going to get harder for me to climb out of.

The way I eventually did climb out of that hole was another example of how playing football has helped me throughout my life. Football got me working out starting in the eighth grade, and it became an ingrained habit. That discipline has pulled me out of the darkness many times. My normal routine is to just start working out. This usually leads to me eating healthier and eventually getting into decent shape. I maintain this routine as long as I can before falling off the wagon again. I wait for my weight and back pain to build up again and then repeat—this is not a very healthy or consistent cycle.

Eating healthy has always been the hardest part for me. If I'm not working out, I'm not eating healthy. I had to get clever to pull myself out of this particular shitstorm I got myself into. I ordered everything I needed to do P90X: dumbbells, a pull-up bar, a yoga mat, even the P90X recovery drink—whatever I could possibly get to eliminate any excuses I might make to push it off even longer. I had everything needed for the workouts, I went and got everything outlined in the nutrition guide, and I couldn't make any more excuses. It was time to get right.

The only other issue was how to fit working out into my schedule. I was cutting down trees for eight hours a day in the snow, and by the time I got off work, I was spent. The only way to make my workout plan stick was to commit to exercising before work. I woke up at 3:00 a.m. each day, prepared whatever was on the P90X nutrition guide for the day, and did the workout in my room. I had to make sure I arrived at work by 5:30 a.m. each morning to have everything ready for the crew when they started at 6:00 a.m.

I went pretty slowly with the workouts in the beginning. Most of the time, I just went through the motions to get acclimated to each movement. My main concern was how my headaches would react. Once I felt safe, I started pushing a little harder each day.

One thing I had to watch out for on the P90X nutrition plan was consuming sufficient calories. I did the recommended workouts, stretching, and ab exercises seven days a week while cutting down trees in the snow or chipping what we had cut down. I was burning way more calories than I was putting into my body. I was losing weight, but it wasn't healthy. I was hungry all the time. My skin turned greenish. It was like I was back in high school, starving myself again. It wasn't good, but I finished the ninety days. I lost forty pounds—the weight I needed to lose plus some—and even though it wasn't the healthiest way to do it, it put me back in control of my back pain and quieted the noise between my ears. I was moving forward again.

Near the end of my run with Jason, we finally sat down and had a real conversation. We both explained how we felt and got everything out on the table. He apologized, and so did I. We were both put in bad positions, and I should've been honest with him from the beginning. If I had been honest, the whole situation might have played out completely differently. He had big plans for the upcoming season, and during that conversation, we decided to attack them together. But our relationship had changed. Working for someone who had treated me so badly when I was down was going to be tough. Plus, he planned to switch me over to a salary and pay me $28,000 per year. After I had busted my ass for him, he was going to slash my pay. It was obvious I had to make a change. So when an assistant opportunity opened at the Liberty Club, a private, twenty-seven-hole facility about forty-five minutes away, I considered it. The club's superintendent, Paul VanLanduit, had a reputation for getting his assistants their first superintendent positions. I had a conversation with Jason about it, and he agreed it would be a great opportunity.

I applied to the Liberty Club and got my first real interview. I dressed up in a suit and tie. I spoke with Paul and the general manager of the club, and I thought it went well. At the end of the interview, I crossed the fingers on both my hands, held them near my chest with a smile, and told Paul how much I would love to work for him. He interviewed five other guys and then called me back in for a second interview. When I got there, instead of interviewing me again, he offered me the job with a salary of almost $40,000 per year! He said the GM and he both agreed I would be a great fit, and he couldn't forget how I had crossed my fingers and told him I wanted the job. My advice to anyone interviewing is that while you don't want to seem desperate, showing enthusiasm for a role doesn't hurt.

I'll never forget my time with Jason. Even though things weren't the greatest toward the end, I'm very thankful for all he taught me. He showed me how to harness my work ethic and the energy I have toward life and use them in my profession. He made me love what I do for a living. Not all lessons are learned easily, but I learned these lessons from him.

CHAPTER 15

THE LIBERTY CLUB

FINDING CONFIDENCE

I SECURED AN APARTMENT NEAR THE LIBERTY CLUB. NOW, it was time to figure out why Paul was so highly respected in our industry. My role working for him was completely different than what I had done for Jason. Jason taught me how to build tee boxes and bunkers, how to change site lines, and basically all the construction aspects of a golf course. Paul taught me how to be a superintendent. He had a program in place, and I had to run it to the best of my ability with our available resources. He allowed his assistants to run the show, which essentially let me act as the superintendent. He'd only correct me when I slipped up. Paul taught me to look through his eyes so I could be an extension of him on the course. He allowed me to go to Grounds and Greens Committee meetings at the club, which is a pivotal part of communicating with members and gathering feedback. He allowed me and encouraged me to interact with members and build relationships. This was an entirely new part of my profession I needed to learn.

The only problem when I first started was my finances. I thought I would be able to support myself easily as a single male making $40,000 a year. But my monthly expenses were insane. (My student loans crippled me when I got out of college.) Between rent, utility bills, gas costs, student loans, and a car payment, my salary didn't cover all my costs. I started losing money each month, and the debt on my credit cards increased. Using credit cards was the only way for me to get by each month. Then, after about eight months of losing money, I lucked out. One of the assistant pros from the club moved to a new job, which left our other assistant pro in need of a roommate. Even luckier, a member at the club had a few separate homes he was trying to sell, and he let us live in them until they sold. He barely charged us anything for rent—$165 a month compared to the $850 a month I had been paying. Plus, now the utilities were split! I was able to start digging myself out of the financial hole I had created on my credit cards and put every spare penny toward paying off my student loans.

I could not believe the house I got to live in. It was unreal—a huge ranch home with a basement that sat on more than three acres of land and backed up to a seventy-five-acre lake. The homeowner left a little plastic boat down near the dock, which we used to fish in every chance we got. My roommate and I both worked a lot of hours, so whenever we got to use the boat, the experience was that much sweeter. The house was so large we even put a Ping-Pong table in one of the living rooms. It was a fun time.

Meanwhile, my exercise and diet regimen was losing its thrill. I had done P90X three or four more times since I first tried it (but I boosted my calorie intake to do it more safely than the first time), and I was over it. P90X was great—it checked all my boxes, quieted the noise that came along with life, and kept my back from chronically hurting—but it was getting boring. I wanted to try something new, and I finally had the money, time, and confidence to try CrossFit, the popular workout method that promotes high-intensity, functional exercises in a "box gym." I signed up.

I liked having a different workout each day and getting to do squats and Olympic lifting. The workouts kept me engaged and challenged me while also allowing me to compete against everyone else who did the workout each day. First, I was required to go to introductory classes to learn the proper form for all the movements. I liked it, but the hardest part was making that last leap and joining the regular classes. It was intimidating, but I'm so glad I did. It changed the way I think about fitness and nutrition.

The fad inside the CrossFit community is eating "paleo," or "the caveman diet," which involves eating only food cavemen had available to them (meat, fish, vegetables, fruits, nuts and seeds, and healthy fats). I tried this diet, and it made a huge difference in the way I felt and performed. After following it strictly for four weeks, I felt better than I ever had before. I gained an amazing amount of energy. My attitude was much better. I was able to get out of my head more. The minor aches and pains I normally felt were gone. I didn't understand how it worked, but it was doing something I had never felt before. I'm a big believer in worrying only about what you can control. Eating clean and working out allowed me to get out of my head, and I was able to control my back pain. Now, I had new weapons to fight my never-ending battle. Having this advantage raised my confidence level tremendously.

Shortly after starting CrossFit, I approached Paul with an

idea to address a common frustration in the golf course industry. All golf club members either mow their lawns or pay someone to mow their lawns, which makes them think they're experts in turf. As a superintendent, this is very aggravating. You could be doing everything perfectly on the course according to one member but a horrendous job according to the next member. A great quote from Roy Williams, the UNC men's basketball coach, sums it up best: "Being a college basketball coach and a golf course superintendent must be the easiest jobs in the world because everyone thinks they can do it better than you."

My idea was to put together a course maintenance standards book that clearly outlined our goals and practices on the course. It would address mowing heights, green speeds, how many times bunkers are raked per week, how often divots are filled, and every other practice done on the course. All content would be approved by the Grounds and Greens Committee. Having such a book would help protect the superintendent's job. With it, if members wanted you to change a particular practice, the change would have to be voted on by the committee and updated in the standards book before becoming reality instead of merely suggested to the superintendent. This would allow the superintendent to focus on the objectives outlined in the standards book without having to field conflicting standards suggestions and put the superintendent in control of his or her own job. Having a standards book made for one less headache I had to worry about. Creating it helped me follow one of my mottos: don't worry about what's out of your control, or at least try not to.

Paul loved the idea. When we presented it to our committee members, they loved it too. A digital copy went to all members and potential members so they knew exactly what to expect from course conditioning. Soon, other departments were asked to create standards for their areas as well. Having a standards book helped each department become much more organized, and the more organized we were, the less stress we had. It simplified things for everyone.

My goal at the Liberty Club was to be a superintendent by the time I was twenty-seven years old. Paul's program for getting superintendent jobs for his assistants was on a three-year rotation. In addition to helping his assistants advance, his program found Paul new, young, ambitious turf guys every three years or so. That meant he had a consistent source of new ideas and practices. We all need to stay students of our professions, and this approach worked great for Paul. Paul and I spoke about every job opportunity that arose and whether or not it would be a good fit for me. I had a few shots during interviews but fell short in the competitive market. Finally, toward the end of my third season with Paul, a job opened at Snowdrift Golf Club in the transition zone. It was ranked thirty-seventh in the country in *Golf Digest's* Top 100 courses. It would be a great club to have on my résumé. The job had opened a year or so earlier, and I flirted with it but ended up not getting it. I was on the fence about the job, but after a discussion with Paul, we decided I needed to take another shot at applying.

The process of going after a new job is no small feat because of the many qualified applicants applying for the same position. The process includes phone call after phone call, polishing your résumé, going to see this and that person, and doing everything you can to put yourself in a position to succeed. The owner of Snowdrift Golf Club was William Hudson, and his son-in-law Owen happened to be a member at Liberty. I asked my pro-shop staff to tell me the next time Owen came to the course. Not only did they do that, but the head pro, Lou Mickelson, spoke to Owen about what a great guy I was on and off the course. Lou has helped me with potential jobs time and time again; he's the best. But I found out that impressing the golf course architect who designed Snowdrift, Don Grigsby, would be critical to landing the position.

With Paul by my side, I called Don. The phone conversation was not going well. He thought I might be a good fit, but he really wanted an established superintendent to fill the role. Paul took the phone from me to talk to Don himself. Paul explained my role at Liberty was, for all intents and purposes, that of a superintendent. He explained what he'd done for other assistants who were, at that point, superintendents flourishing around the Chicagoland area. By the end of the conversation, Paul had Don convinced I was the perfect fit. I had to get my résumé to Don as soon as possible so he could put it in front of Mr. Hudson. Normally, it could take a week or two to hear something after an interview, but I received a phone call from Mr. Hudson two days later. We had a brief conversation, and he offered me the job. I tried to negotiate a better salary, but he wasn't having any of it and tried to end our conversation. I backed off and accepted the position. I would have housing and a vehicle, but I wasn't getting a big raise or any insurance or retirement plan. On the bright side, I would be twenty-eight years old and a golf course superintendent of the thirty-seventh-ranked golf course in the country!

I didn't stop there. I continued to make calls to anyone who had anything to do with Snowdrift previously. I called past employees, sales reps, and contractors. My goal was to limit surprises going in. I wanted to be prepared for anything. After hours of phone calls, my expectation was to go down and knock it out of the park for two to three years until I could find a good job. Snowdrift was an unbelievable course but not a good job for a superintendent. Having superintendent experience at the thirty-seventh-ranked course in the country on my résumé would open up a lot of doors.

The final part of the job-change process was to find Paul a great assistant to replace me. I was leaving one month before the season ended, and I was able to set Paul up with my good friend Jack. He came in and didn't miss a beat. Paul got him his first superintendent job two years later.

CHAPTER 16

SNOWDRIFT

PERSEVERING IN THE FACE OF ADVERSITY

THE SIGNIFICANCE OF GETTING THE SUPERINTENDENT position at Snowdrift Golf Club didn't truly hit me until the first time I met Mr. Hudson. He had an office near the Liberty Club and wanted to meet me face to face to give me a truck. We didn't talk for long before he walked me outside and pointed at a new, black, four-door F-150. I was trembling and could barely speak. Once I drove the truck into my driveway, the floodgates opened. I had a new truck and a superintendent job, and I couldn't hold back the tears of joy and accomplishment. All my hard work had paid off. The long, hard hours of backbreaking work outside in the elements, the effort of putting myself through college, the brain injuries, making it out of that drug house I called home—I had overcome all of it. Guys like me weren't expected to make it out of their unstable environments. I was supposed to be trash, an addict. I was supposed to kill myself or be locked away in jail. But I had made it out, and it was because of my ability to keep moving forward. I never used setbacks as excuses to quit. My drive never stopped; I was determined I would not become my parents.

Let me describe Snowdrift. Imagine driving through corn country, flat cornfields as far as the eye can see. Suddenly, you see an immaculately landscaped entrance with a front gate similar to the one in the original *Jurassic Park* movie. The driveway is one lane of concrete with a split-rail fence on both sides, always freshly painted. A row of snowdrift crabapple trees line either side of the driveway, spaced twenty yards apart for about three hundred yards. The concrete path meanders down into a river that you drive through before the ascent up to Bill's log mansion and the golf course. It is a little oasis in the middle of nothing. The amount of earth that was moved to build the course is insane. Millions of dollars' worth of rock features are scattered throughout the course, with ever-flowing waterfalls and creeks built into the landscape. To say I was overwhelmed would be the understatement of the century.

But I knew I was prepared. I found out the mechanic at Snowdrift, Forest, was more of a caretaker of the property. Bill rarely visited the course—perhaps two or three times a year during my tenure—so Forest was Bill's eyes and ears. Another person I learned had a lot of clout with Forest was Becky, the bookkeeper for Bill's golf course and farmland. Both Forest and Becky were behind the firings of the last two superintendents. One was fired after six months, and the other even more quickly. I knew I had to be extremely careful around them both, but I also wanted to develop a great relationship with them to help me accomplish my goals. They had to trust me. I was also prepared because I had evaluated the course a few weeks earlier. To my surprise, there was a lot of dead turf. The dead grass on the greens was most surprising. Three holes had large areas that needed to be addressed. I had taken picture after picture of the dead turf during my visit to protect my ass.

The first month was pretty simple. Bill still wanted *Golf Digest* raters to play so we could accumulate as many ratings as possible. The rankings come out every two years. I just had to dial in the course in its current condition to the best of its ability. Once the course was closed to raters, the fun would start, including sodding out dead areas on greens, roughs, fairways, and tees. I would need to renovate all the landscape beds, which were about eight years past their prime. They were all overgrown and would not be acceptable at any course, much less at the thirty-seventh-ranked course in the country. I had to pay particularly close attention to the landscaping between the ninth green and the first tee because it was the players' first visual. Island after island of overgrown landscaping was mixed with huge waterfalls, and a large cougar statue stood guard over the biggest one. Despite the amount of work needed, renovating and repairing the course was going to be the easy part. All my headaches would soon come from Becky, Forest, and trying to communicate my master plan to Bill.

At any course, you're only as good as your crew. So, for the first year and half, I spent most of my time training the staff on how to be most efficient. We were in the middle of nowhere, so recruiting staff members was hard. Plus, the course did not pay overtime, and our normal schedule was fifty-six hours a week: eight-hour days, seven days a week. We ramped up the number of hours during projects and when we had golfers. In-season, I worked sixty to eighty hours a week because I ended up being in charge of the entire property, not just the golf course. An added layer of difficulty to hiring and keeping staff was the policy that if someone missed a punch-in or punch-out, I couldn't change the time to correct the mistake. You heard that right. If an employee worked a thirteen-hour day and forgot to punch out, he would not get compensated for his time. I took extreme pride in fighting for my employees, taking care of them to the best of my ability. Employees forget to punch out; it happens. I fought a good fight with Bill and Becky time and time again to get employees paid, but not once did they allow it. It's a gut punch not being able to care for the people who take care of you. I lost a lot of good (and bad) employees for this reason.

A great benefit of my time at Snowdrift was that I finally earned enough to start saving money for the first time in my life. My student loans had crippled me financially for five years, but I finally had a grasp on them, which felt empowering. Since I used the company truck, I sold my Jeep on Craigslist. I listed it at 8:00 p.m. on a Sunday night and had $7,500 in cash in my hand by 4:00 p.m. the next day. I put every cent toward my loans. The day I paid off my loans (it took seven years) was emotional. There was no huge celebration—I simply made the last payment online, alone in my apartment. Then I stared off into space with tears of joy running down my face. I was happier than when I graduated. I had bet everything on myself and won. I finally felt like I was making progress in my life. I could not wait to call Uncle Noah and Aunt Grace, who helped make it possible. With my student loans gone, I was able to start saving for retirement. After doing a little research, I started an E-Trade account, opened a Roth IRA, and bought some blue-chip stocks like Apple. I was thrilled to be able to prepare for my future, even if I was getting a bit of a late start.

One of the best things I learned at Snowdrift was how to provide excellent customer service. I met golfers in the parking lot with their golf carts for each round of golf. I outlined a rough itinerary and did whatever I could to make the day the best experience of their lives. After all, each guest was screened by Bill and Becky before they were approved to play at $800 per person per round. I loaded them into their carts, answered any questions, and told them about the property. Then, I took them to the clubhouse, and we started the nearly half-mile trek to the driving range, going up and down some of the steepest concrete cart paths you can imagine. Finally, we reached five small driving-range tees tucked behind hole fifteen, each blocked from the others by mounding and landscaping for an unbothered experience.

I had set up three pyramids of golf balls on each tee, perfectly spaced from one another, with the Snowdrift logo facing out on each golf ball. I stayed at the chipping area until the guests were done at the driving range and ready to play. Then, I escorted them back to the clubhouse and took them to the first tee. I loaded up their coolers with whatever refreshments they desired and let them know what time lunch or dinner would be ready. The meals we served the guests were just as unique as the course. A caterer named Harper-Lynn from the nearest town whipped up classic meals, improving them with her own flair. Even if the guests didn't like the course, there was no way they didn't like the food. A unique, amazing meal had to be worth something for a person rating the course.

My time at Snowdrift was all about providing each guest with the best possible experience. If they asked me to play with them, I always said yes, for at least a few holes. Some groups asked me to stay the entire eighteen holes, which I did, despite what else I needed to do. They wanted me to answer their questions about the property and Bill and give advice on how to play each hole. I thoroughly enjoyed entertaining the guests. Sometimes, I also played tour guide and showed people the property. Whatever I needed to do, I understood it was all part of the job. Entertaining was something very unique to Snowdrift. The mindset of creating a world-class experience for every guest is something I will carry with me for the rest of my career.

Snowdrift was so amazing that even though I had planned on staying only a couple years, until I could get a better long-term job, I quickly began to wonder if I could turn the Snowdrift job into the career job I wanted. I researched whether or not anyone at the farm or golf course had ever received health insurance or retirement benefits. The answer was no, not even the first superintendent, who was there for ten years. I soon determined that making Snowdrift my long-term plan had too many drawbacks.

The first drawback was I was making only $5,000 more a year than I was as an assistant. I did have a vehicle and free housing, but the apartment was small, was too close to neighbors, and had too many issues for me to live in it for an extended period of time.

The next drawback was I didn't have as much authority as I needed when it came to the financial aspect of the job. This was frustrating because I prided myself on documenting every purchase, budgeting well, and keeping expenses within $1 million per year, which is incredible for a 350-acre property. What made this property more expensive to manage than most was it had all cool-season grass in the transition zone; the natural environments for its grass varieties were a lot cooler and less humid than the environment they were planted in. That meant more chemicals and cultural practices were needed to keep the turf healthy. Given this, producing results for under $1 million each season was unreal.

The hardest part of managing the budget was I didn't have an operating budget to work within. Instead, Bill required I submit a "budget" to him each year. But the budget was only the purchase requisitions he signed that year. I had to fight for some of the most basic things I needed to operate the course, and many he would deny. That was how he ran all his companies. For example, every year at his other golf course, Devil's Creek, he would not sign the purchase requisition for the operating system that handled all tee times and purchases at the club. Every club needs a basic system for daily operations. The pro at the club would have to go back and forth with him for sometimes nearly a month before he would get approval to operate. When you are trying to run a company for someone, but your requests for basic needs keep getting shot down, it takes a toll. I saw the life and passion drained from the faces of the people who worked for Bill. I could not let that happen to me. After my first season with Bill, I saw how not having a true budget put a strain on everyone and everything. So, at the end of the season, I spent weeks putting together an operating budget with graphs and justifications for purchases. It was as clearly communicated as I could make it. I presented it to him and received a quick no, even though the budget was under $1 million. All I wanted was to be able to operate within that budget instead of having to request a signed purchase requisition each time I needed something.

Another big drawback of staying at Snowdrift was dealing with Becky, who had been with Bill for a while and protected her territory with a ferocity many have never witnessed. She caused many of Bill's workers to quit. Even contractors would refuse work because they didn't want to deal with her wrath. That says a lot in a small town where there are not many jobs available. I knew this going in, but it was still frustrating. I believe I particularly drove her crazy because I was a young, enthusiastic person who loved what he did. She would go after me by distorting something petty and getting Bill all fired up about it. Then, he would come after me, I would explain the situation (backed up by Forest behind closed doors), and everything would be fine until Becky tossed her next monkey wrench to bog down our well-oiled machine. Constantly defending your integrity when you have done nothing wrong is infuriating. For example, she frequently lost signed purchase requisitions and insisted they were never turned in. Becky fought us tooth and nail saying she had never received them. Forest and I kept track of how many times we gave her the same signed purchase requisitions. The most we ever had to resubmit was six times. Printing off another copy and handing it to her was a lot easier than trying to argue.

Other examples of Becky's shenanigans include the time she "forgot" to pay the utility bill on the company apartment I lived in on Super Bowl weekend. She would not fix the leak in my bedroom ceiling that I told her about a half dozen times. She told Bill lies like saying my crew foreman just drove around in a cart and didn't do any work all day. She forced me into firing my irrigation tech—not what you want to have happen going into a new job with no as-builts. That meant no maps for the irrigation system. If I had an irrigation leak, I had to go on the Easter egg hunt from hell to find the valve that turned off the water. Sometimes, we would have to shut off the pump house to stop the water flow. Yet, she got rid of the one tenured employee who knew where the majority of the valves were, all for a non-work-related issue—he had gotten into a shouting match with his girlfriend, the police showed up, and he got a noise warning. She blew it out of proportion to Bill, and he made me fire the employee directly after hearing the news.

Becky's tactics were harder to deal with than they might have been because of another drawback: communicating with Bill was extremely difficult. He was great to talk with in person; he and I usually were on the same page. But he worked mostly at his office nearly six hours away, so face-to-face conversations were rare. We had to communicate through a fax machine most of the time—not the easiest way to justify my actions against Becky's complaints. When faxing didn't work, I had to call him. Sometimes, Bill would start off brash because Becky had worked him up so much, but we were always both on the same page by the end of our conversations. I told him my side, and he understood I was not trying to get into a pissing match with anyone. I loved my job; I just wanted to be allowed to do it.

The biggest and most disappointing drawback about the job kept playing out: I was not able to take care of my employees. A good example was when I reached out to my old WKU advisor to see if he had any graduating turf students who were looking for an assistant role. I lucked out and lined up a great kid named Hanes. After I went to war with Bill and Becky to get him a discount on an apartment and a decent wage, he was hired. Everything was going smoothly that winter as we geared up for the following season until Becky told Bill my employees were working too many hours. I had to cut everyone's hours down to twenty-four a week. Hanes couldn't make rent on his apartment anymore and was put in a horrible position. He had to take a different job with a more reliable wage. That was one of the worst feelings of failure I have ever experienced as a supervisor. I brought a young, smart, bright-eyed kid into his first assistant job, and I couldn't take care of him.

Strangely, despite all these drawbacks, I really enjoyed my job. I loved doing course projects, building bunkers and tee boxes, and doing cool things like running large machinery. We had everything at Snowdrift. The maintenance shop was the best I had ever worked in, and the equipment was top-notch. I was running a top 100 course, maybe the most exclusive course in the country, yet I knew I had to leave in a few years or the fire that had been lit inside of me for my profession would slowly die. Occasionally, I still toyed with the idea of starting a side business or buying property to earn enough money on the side to afford to stay at Snowdrift forever. But I just didn't have enough free time to do that with what the course demanded, and there was no future for me there anyway. Everyone who stayed either quit or was fired over some bullshit. The few guys who stayed until retirement age had nothing to show for it, even when they thought something was coming their way. When thoughts of staying crept in, I'd remind myself of the other employees' drained passion and the fact that there was no future there, which kept me focused on my long-term plan, allowing me to keep moving forward.

CHAPTER 17

MY FIRST LOVE

Cori

THE MOST IMPORTANT THING THAT CAME FROM MY TIME at Snowdrift was Cori—a German shorthaired pointer (GSP) I purchased within months of starting there. I had always wanted a dog, but being an assistant superintendent didn't allow much spare time. I had planned for years to get a Labrador retriever as soon as I got my first superintendent role. Then one year, on my annual Thanksgiving duck-hunting trip with the Quinn family, someone brought a twelve-week-old GSP. It was the cutest little dog I had ever seen. It napped with me a few times and took a poop in my shoe; I was sold. I knew I wanted one someday.

Once I had Cori, the responsibility of owning a dog hit me. The realization that I was everything to this little animal was scary. If I didn't feed her, she had nothing to eat. If I didn't provide her water, she had nothing to drink. I was responsible for showing her right from wrong and making sure she never felt neglected. Owning her triggered a bunch of old memories of raising Gunner and the way my parents raised me. I feared I wasn't able to properly care for a dog. Maybe I wasn't capable of overseeing another life. My parents had made choices that were not good for my well-being, and I was scared I might make the same mistakes. Perhaps neglect was in my blood. I had been too gung ho about getting a dog to entertain doubts before I got Cori. Now, she was my responsibility, and I had to do whatever I could to set her up for success. That was my job as a "pawrent."

I knew Cori was going to have a great life as a golf-course dog. She went to work with me every day and ran around "her" course, protecting it from geese and pesky squirrels. She is fun loving and incredibly smart. Watching her learn blows me away; I can see her listening to every word and trying to learn. Plus, I never have to worry about her hurting anyone or anything unless she thinks I'm in danger. She has been crucial to my mental and emotional progress. Having the responsibility of putting her well-being above mine did so much for my growth. She became my best friend, a true companion.

Some may say, "She's just a dog," but this dog stayed with me every day at work and at home. She was a valuable part of my job and always there for me at Snowdrift in the middle of nowhere, where I knew no one. To say the job, Becky, Bill, and Forest didn't get to me would be a lie. I felt overwhelmed and lost more times than I can count during my time at Snowdrift. Thoughts of self-doubt and pity often crept in. It felt like the deck was stacked against me. When Becky made trouble, I had the same feelings from my past when my mom would yell at me and dismantle someone because the person made me happy. But Cori was always right there, cheering me up with her little, wagging tail. Breakdown after breakdown, I was ready to toss in the towel, but instead, I talked to Cori. She was my friend who was always there to listen. She was my shoulder to cry on. I could depend on her. She quickly turned into family for me. I know at some point I'm going to outlive her, and the thought of her not being with me every day is soul crushing. She's the first living creature to put my well-being above her own. If she thinks I'm in danger, something clicks in her, and she protects me with every ounce of her being. I love that dog so much.

When Cori was about eight months old, she and I went to check something out on the back side of the course. On my way back, I lost her. That wasn't unusual; she often stopped to sniff something here or there and met me back at the shop. But this time, she didn't show up. I went back out to search for her but couldn't find her. When I returned to the shop, I found her lying down in front of the office door. Blood was everywhere. When she stood up, her left hind leg dangled in the air, and it looked shredded just above her paw. I carefully scooped her up, laid her in the back seat of my truck, and headed to the vet.

Everyone at the vet's office knew Cori, and they were heartbroken to see her in that condition. The accident had shredded nearly all the tendons and ligaments in her ankle. We had two options: put her in a cast for six to eight weeks and let it heal, or fuse the bones together. I chose the cast; she would lose her range of motion with a fusion, and I didn't want her to have basically a stilt for a leg. The doctor decided to try a soft cast. I suggested a hard cast because all GSPs want to do is run. I didn't think a soft cast would limit her enough considering she needed to be immobile for it to heal. The doctor disagreed. I tried to persuade her by using myself as an example. I had a soft cast once when I broke my hand, and even though I'm a human and understood why I shouldn't use that hand, I constantly took it off, taped my fingers together, and did whatever I pleased. My hand didn't heal until they forced me not to use it by putting me in a hard cast. I pleaded, "She's a dog. All she wants to do is run. A soft cast will not stop her." My pleading did nothing.

After six weeks in the soft cast with little improvement, the doctor asked for a second opinion from an expert in the field. The expert suggested using a hard cast to limit Cori's movement, but it was too late by that time. I wish I would've fought harder for a hard cast. Instead, I trusted the expert, and as a result, Cori had to stay in the soft cast another eight weeks. Every time I took her in for a checkup, they peeled off the cast while Cori licked the floor in pain. It was amazing how well she behaved despite being in so much pain, but it was hard to see her suffer. I would hold her to help keep her calm while the doctor and her assistants did their thing, but the results were very disappointing. Eventually, her leg healed enough to allow her to run, but when she's too active, it still swells up and hurts her too much to put any weight on it. She's a tough, good girl and will have to deal with this for the rest of her life. This experience strengthened my belief that instead of just trusting the experts, I should trust my instincts more and stand up for what I believe.

I didn't know what happened to Cori until a few days after the incident, when an employee approached me in tears, confessing she had accidentally run over Cori with a utility vehicle. She thought Cori was dead and was afraid she would lose her job if she told me. But she felt horrible and decided I needed to know what happened. I told her it wasn't her fault. When she was that young, Cori often ran in front of vehicles. If a driver's attention lapsed for a second, it would've been easy to run her over. I was grateful the employee told me what happened, even though it was hard to hear.

I'm married now and have a child, and even my beautiful wife jokes that she knows Cori is number one. But in all seriousness, Cori helped pull me through tough times, and in return, I'm providing her with the best life a dog can live.

CHAPTER 18

HEALTH ISSUES

FINDING ANSWERS

I DIDN'T HAVE MEDICAL INSURANCE BECAUSE SNOWDRIFT didn't provide any, and I couldn't afford private insurance. Obamacare had just come out, penalizing the noninsured with a fine, but the plans were unaffordable. Like all working-class citizens, I had to choose between the lesser of two evils: go broke paying for insurance, or take a chance on having no major medical issues. I chose the latter because it was cheaper to pay the fine and pay for medical expenses out of pocket for me.

Shortly after Cori's accident, I had my own medical issues. I thought I had a virus that would run its course in a week or so, but after three weeks, I wasn't feeling any better. I lost thirteen pounds, and my energy was spent. I could barely make it through each day at work. I knew a doctor would be expensive, but I wasn't improving, and I needed to get better, so I sought medical care. The doctor said he knew exactly what was wrong. He prescribed a medication and told me I should start feeling better in a few days. I gave it a week, but my weight continued to drop, and I had even less energy to get through each day. Being a golf course superintendent demands a lot from you physically, and getting through each day was becoming more and more of a struggle. My symptoms were nausea, weakness, loss of appetite, abdominal pain, diarrhea, and a feeling of hunger despite eating. Feeling hungry after stuffing myself was one of the most awkward feelings I've ever had.

I went back in and saw a different doctor. He was confused about why his counterpart had prescribed the medication he had on my previous visit. The new doctor didn't believe anything was seriously wrong with me; he told me to give it more time and my symptoms would go away. I left feeling disheartened. I had lost eighteen pounds by then and had no energy. I felt guilty because I couldn't keep up at work. Instead of setting an example, I was letting my crew down. All of it was taking a heavy toll on me mentally and physically.

I couldn't continue in my condition. It was up to me to find out what the hell was going on. I am very in tune with my body, and I felt like something was inside me. When I got home, I googled all my symptoms, and the word "parasite" kept popping up. It made perfect sense once I learned more. Not only was I out in the elements all day, but sometimes I worked in stagnant water, where parasites live. Or I could have gotten a parasite from some "iffy" bacon I ate just before I got sick. *This is it*, I thought. I went back to the doctor and told him what I discovered. He disagreed. I asked, "Could you just prescribe medicine that would cure me if I do have a parasite?" He refused. I said, "Look, Doc, I don't have insurance. I'm paying for this out of pocket. I'm not making this up; something is wrong." But he thought it was some phantom sickness I was imagining.

"Pissed" doesn't begin to describe the anger I felt after that visit. When I got home, I researched which parasite is most often associated with my symptoms. I learned I most likely had a parasite from the undercooked bacon I ate, and I found the drug I needed. However, I could not purchase it without a prescription. As I searched for the drug online, one of the links I found was for dogs. The dog version of the medicine didn't require a prescription. I was desperate, so I continued to investigate. I found that the medications for humans and animals both come from the same facility and are basically the same. I looked up the dosage usually prescribed for someone my height and weight, and then I bought what my local pet store carried and ordered the rest online. I was supposed to take it once and then again two weeks later to clean up anything the first dose missed. I remember standing between my kitchen and living room at my apartment, medication in hand, saying, "I can't keep living like this." I was really nervous, but I gathered my courage, said, "Fuck it!" and downed it.

My stomach cramps intensified that night, but I had read that was normal. When I woke up the next morning, I had energy for the first time in nearly eight weeks. Trying that medication was a little wild, and I didn't think I was out of the woods yet. But that whole day I felt fine; my energy level did not get depleted. I felt good the entire two weeks before my second dose, but I still took it, just in case.

I was glad I had listened to my gut instincts. The parasite medication was a simple fix, but the doctor was totally against it, probably because it was my suggestion, not his. He refused to listen to me just like the vet refused to listen about the hard cast for Cori's leg. I think some doctors feel superior to their patients, so if you question their diagnoses, they fight tooth and nail to prove they are right. In both instances, I tried to make my case in the most nonthreatening way I could, but it didn't matter.

Their minds were made up, and there was nothing I could say to change them. This was another example that sometimes you just have to take matters into your own hands. No one can tell you how you feel. Finding a cure for your problems, mentally and physically, is ultimately up to you.

Meanwhile, my chronic back pain was getting worse. I had obviously stopped working out during my illness. I decided that winter to see a specialist and have my back checked out to get a better understanding of what was wrong with it. I was open to surgery or whatever was necessary to improve it. I had been doing CrossFit for almost three years by that time, and four times I had to stop for six to ten weeks to let my back recover because I had pushed too hard. I wasn't just missing workouts; I was in horrendous pain. The pain would first shoot down my legs, a little bit farther down my left leg than my right. As time passed, the pain would creep back up my legs and settle in my back. At this point, I knew I was three to four weeks away from feeling better. My back would feel extremely delicate, as if a nine-inch section of my lower spine had been shattered and placed back together, and the whole area felt bruised.

The back pain was bad enough, but every time I stopped working out to heal, my entire routine also went out the window. I lost any progress I had made at the gym, my diet took a turn for the worse, and the normal stresses of life started getting to me more and staying in my head longer. My anxiety and self-doubt would start circling again. Continuing this pattern was hurting me physically and mentally and preventing me from moving forward. Nothing drives me more insane than being stagnant. Going to a specialist and understanding exactly what was going on was a way I could take back control.

The orthopedic doctor was surprised when he saw me. He expected me to be obese, like the majority of his patients. I explained what was going on with my back and why I was concerned. I described the movements that hurt my back the most, in particular, holding weight out in front of me. After my last few medical experiences, I was amazed that the doctor actually listened to me. I could tell he was digesting the information I gave him, which was a nice change from the way Cori's vet and my last doctor treated me.

Next, we went over the MRI scans previously taken of my back. He pulled them up on his computer and gave me a simplified explanation of the problem so I could understand. I had four bulging discs and a narrow spinal column. Working out caused the discs to protrude into my spinal column and pinch my nerves, which was causing the pain. I asked him about surgery, and he told me that was a last resort. If I could manage the pain without surgery, surgery shouldn't be an option. We came up with a game plan. First, I had to identify what specific workout moves hurt my back and then not do them. Judging what was normal pain and what was back-injury pain was going to be difficult. I needed to walk the fine line of pushing myself but not injuring myself. Second, he prescribed a steroid in case I misjudged and injured my back again. In that case, I was to take it immediately, along with a high dose of ibuprofen every four to six hours, to alleviate the swelling and recover faster. Third and finally, he prescribed muscle relaxers to help me sleep since pain had been waking me up frequently during the night. The muscle relaxers allowed more rest, which would also speed the recovery process. Having a game plan that cut my recovery time from six to ten weeks down to four to six weeks was a relief. What helped the most was knowing I had control again and the confidence that came with it.

I also asked the orthopedic doctor for advice on my left knee, which I had injured a year and a half earlier when my leg flared out in an awkward position while I was doing power snatches. As soon as it happened, my knee swelled up and got hot. The swelling went around the front of my kneecap and wrapped around the back, forming a ring. It hurt, but I put a knee sleeve on and finished the workout. After that, my knee constantly hurt, especially when doing exercises that pulled it. Pushing into my knee was fine. After I explained this to the doctor, he said it sounded like a partial tear in my meniscus. Again, he did not recommend surgery. He explained surgery creates scar tissue, which could lead to fluid gathering around the area, which would eventually cause more pain.

While I had hoped surgery would be the magical cure for both my back and knee, having a game plan was still empowering. Employing a self-govern was going to be the hardest part. If I could follow the game plan properly, I could shorten the recovery periods and thus the periods of unhealthy living that were detrimental to my mental and physical health.

I hear people talk about the noise in their heads and the inner demons they fight. I think having a screwed-up childhood significantly impacts that battle between the ears. I know we all have unique challenges, but I suspect people who had traumatic childhoods have a bigger amplifier for that noise. In my case, I also must have a backup generator because the noise never stops. But that just means I can't quit either. I can't let those demons catch me slipping because when they do, they're relentless. I almost let them get me in my childhood home in Henderson, Kentucky. I was crying myself to sleep each night trying to think of ways to end the suffering. I haven't had suicidal thoughts in a long time, but I know what my depression and dark thoughts can lead to, and it terrifies me. Those who have been suicidal in the past are more likely to experience suicidal thoughts in the future. I've been a prisoner in my mind before and walked through a good portion of my life in a haze. Peeking my head above the surface, coming up for air in brief stints, has allowed me to keep going. I've learned to use a healthy diet and exercise to fight back against the demons. This strategy doesn't always mute my dark thoughts, but at least it lowers the volume. Now, I'm starting to stay above the surface for longer periods of time, allowing me to make greater progress in my life.

CHAPTER 19

MOVING FORWARD ONCE MORE

AFTER THE ORTHOPEDIC DOCTOR VISIT, I WAS MOVING forward again. I was still working at Snowdrift but putting the full-court press on any good job that opened up. I got a sniff here and there, but nothing had fallen into place yet. Bill was losing interest in the course. He still wanted it immaculate for all guests, but he was visiting less and less often. During my last season, I don't think he went on the course once. He even lost interest in the strawberry farm he had asked me to start. (I had never grown strawberries, but when Bill asked me to do this for him, I wasn't going to say no.)

When the course was originally built, the concrete company Bill hired had idle time between pouring cart paths. Instead of letting them leave to go to other jobs while they waited to pour the next cart path, Bill kept them busy by having them pour rows of concrete in a field. He asked one of the previous superintendents to plant strawberries in between each concrete row, but the superintendent let them die before he put them in the ground and blamed it on deer eating them. It wasn't a great excuse, but with Bill not being on the property and being so busy, he eventually let the excuse pass. (That superintendent must have been smarter than me!)

One day, I discovered two thousand strawberry plants of five different varieties at my front door with no explanation. I called around and eventually got in touch with Bill, who told me he had ordered the plants because he wanted me to start growing strawberries. I researched how to grow them, called the distributor they were purchased from, and got started. We lined the entire plot with a permeable weed fabric and installed an irrigation system. One of my employees' full-time job was pulling weeds in the strawberry field all season. The first year, we even picked off all the flowers because Bill requested it. He said it would help them get established so we could start harvesting the next year. At least I can say I was well rounded thanks to Snowdrift.

During the middle of my third season, Bill hired a management company to run another one of his courses. There are some good management companies out there, but this was not one of them. These guys had a horrible reputation. They had changed their name three or four times by the time they approached Bill. No matter how many times Bill said it wouldn't affect me, I knew at some point the management company would take over Snowdrift as well. The writing was on the wall at that point. I had to find a way out.

Bill asked me to give the owner of the management company a tour of Snowdrift. I quickly understood why the company had such a bad reputation. Obviously, the owner's philosophy had nothing to do with what was best for the course. I've not really talked turf throughout this book, but I believe a conversation I had with that snake about fungicides highlights how little he valued course conditions. Fungicides are used preventively and curatively to kill turfgrass diseases, which can kill the grass. I told him I used Daconil Action on greens. He responded, "Oh, if you use Daconil Action, you shouldn't ever need wetting agents; it's the same thing."

My bullshit-o-meter was already going off, but this broke it. Wetting agents condition the soil to different water-holding capacities. Daconil Action has nothing to do with the soil. He tried to back his argument by telling me the action part in the fungicide acibenzolar accomplished the same objective. Acibenzolar triggers the plant to prepare for stress. It helps in making a healthier plant and does nothing to the soil.

I let his comments roll off me for a couple hours while showing him the property. I could tell how badly he wanted to manage Snowdrift along with Bill's other golf course, Iron Horse, and potentially Bill's resort in Wisconsin. My run at Snowdrift had to be over soon. This snake was going to do whatever it took to get in there. I had done my research on him and his company, and they were known for going into clubs and undercutting the superintendent or general manager by saying they could manage the clubs for less money. They would then bleed out as much money as possible before moving on to the next club (if they weren't kicked out first), leaving the course and facilities in horrible condition and disarray.

As luck would have it, an old friend contacted me about going back to work at the Standard Club, where I did the second half of my internship the summer before my last year of college. He explained that the superintendent, Brian Simpson, whom I'd worked for before and admired, wanted to work only ten more years. If everything went well, I'd learn from him and then take over his role after he retired. The club wanted me to come in and clean up loose ends. They offered me $10,000 more a year, health insurance, a 401(k), and significantly fewer hours and less bullshit. In August, I did a handshake deal with Brian and agreed to make the move in February. Weight lifted off my shoulders instantly. I still did right by Bill until the day I left, but I was no longer stressed about the management company slithering their way into Snowdrift.

I continued with renovations on the course and silently got everything in order for a smooth transition to the Standard Club. Saying goodbye to such a beautiful course and to Bill was going to be hard. He took a chance on me when he hired me. I was an unproven assistant, and he gave me the opportunity to develop into a superintendent. He gave me nearly four years to hone my craft, which allowed me to prepare for my next endeavor.

A few months before I left, Bill came down with his family for the holidays. It was a crapshoot as to whether I would get to see him or talk with him, but I got lucky. He showed up in my office one day, and we got to talking for nearly an hour. During that conversation, he told me the course had gotten better every year I had been there and he appreciated the work I was putting in. I couldn't tell him I was leaving yet because it wasn't close enough to my departure date. Since I didn't know how Bill was going to take the news, I had to be prepared to be fired as soon as I told him. But him telling me the course got better year after year with me there was all I needed to hear to leave with a clean conscience. No matter how he felt about me after I left, at least I knew he was impressed with my work. I would be the first superintendent he didn't fire.

I gave Bill four weeks' notice. I explained the Standard Club had reached out to me with an opportunity I couldn't pass up. He took it well. I thanked him for everything. He allowed me to stay on as long as I wished and said to let him know if I ever wanted to come back. It was great to hear him say that, knowing

I went beyond his expectations. It felt good knowing he was satisfied with my performance.

I appreciated my time at Snowdrift. The best part was I had only one boss, so only one opinion mattered! (At most clubs, every member feels entitled to tell you how the course should look.) I also can say I became more well rounded thanks to Snowdrift. Bill had me do a variety of work, even the unusual and incredibly labor-intensive job of growing strawberries! Most of all, Snowdrift helped me develop my philosophy as a golf course superintendent. There are many ways to skin a cat, and I found the direction I wanted to go. I learned I want to be as environmentally friendly as the budget and consumer allow, and I believe in using as many organic and biological products as possible.

I developed this philosophy by seeing how well it worked at Snowdrift. Using only organic fertilizer and biological controls to get rid of algae and moss in the lakes and layering in the soil reduced the need for other inputs like water, fungicide, and fertilizer. Making the irrigation system more efficient, replacing check valves in the pump station, and learning when and when not to water (and how much to water) dramatically improved the course conditioning. Reducing turning in mowing patterns saved time, burned less fuel, and better preserved the turf. All of these measures protected the environment and lowered the budget without sacrificing quality.

The trick to grass is simple: keep water moving, and get oxygen in the root zone. Anyone who does those two things will be just fine. And remember, it's just grass.

CHAPTER 20

READY FOR OPPORTUNITIES

I BEGAN MY NEW JOB AT THE STANDARD CLUB NEAR CHI-
cago, and it was awesome. One fun thing about the job was I
learned how to embroider. Yes, I embroidered flags for our golf
course and a few friends in the industry. But the best thing that
happened during that time was I started hanging out with my
future wife. After seeing each other for only two weeks, I was
already telling friends I planned to marry Molly. I know that
seems quick, but I already knew her from college; we dated for
a couple months when we were both at WKU. Our feelings were
strong, but neither of us was ready for a serious relationship
back then. She was originally from the Chicago area and had
moved back, so when I moved to Chicago, we met to catch up.
It had been ten years since we dated, but we both knew immediately we had something special. This was the first time in my
life I felt up to the challenge of building a relationship with
someone. I was in a spot emotionally and financially where I
had something to give. There's an old saying: "Are you a fountain or a drain?" I finally felt like a fountain who could be

supportive, giving, and stable. A few months into dating, we decided to move in together. We were both excited about giving the thing between us a chance.

Working at the Standard Club was good, but I was not the one making decisions anymore, and I missed being the superintendent. I never fought with my boss, Brian, and loved working with him, but something was missing. After my first season, I received only a 1.3 percent raise. I expected a lot more, so that didn't feel great, but I didn't go looking for another job. I accepted the situation I had put myself in. But one day, an assistant superintendent friend called and told me about a job he was applying for at Deer Hills Golf and Country Club. It paid well, even more than when the same job had been posted three years earlier. I had seen that post and thought of applying then, but I had not been at Snowdrift long enough.

Molly and I discussed the job opportunity. The move would be a shorter commute for her and put us closer to her family and friends. I gave her a disclaimer before I applied. I told her I felt like I had a 33 percent chance of getting it, which is extremely high in my industry. But, it would require me to be away from home even more than I had been. During the season, I needed to be at work seven days a week. Being a golf course superintendent is more of a lifestyle than a job. Molly would need to spend time with her friends because I wouldn't be able to make it out much. The job would eventually become more flexible, but the beginning would be rough. One of the main reasons I was impressed with Molly was she was making it on her own just fine. She worked at a lawyer's office in downtown Chicago and was willing to put in the work at her job. We had both changed a lot since college, and her independence was attractive. It is also what made our relationship work so well. Molly said, "Go for it."

Before applying, I did my usual research. I spoke with past Deer Hills Golf and Country employees and sales reps who visited the place. I kept hearing about how bad of a place it was to work—the employees were bad, the club's finances were worse, the members were impossible to work for, and the homeowners who lived around the course were brutal. These were all very common complaints, especially after a superintendent had just been let go. In most cases, the superintendent was too stubborn to listen to the membership and failed to communicate what exactly held them back from accomplishing what the membership wanted for the course. My research showed the club paid all their managers well, but it did have a significant amount of debt. A great part of living in our era is all tax information is online. The club was still making money each year, but the interest payments on its debt was handcuffing how much could be put back into the facility. This information proved to me they were not going under any time soon. What surprised me the most was that food and beverage at their clubhouse made money. Most clubs lose money in that department each year, yet the previous year they had earned $270,000 from food and beverage. To put this in perspective, during my last year at the Liberty Club, they lost over $300,000 in that department.

I was not put off by the negative rumors. Members and homeowners being difficult to work with is the same old song. Before he took over at Bear Din Golf Club, Jason heard the same things. He went on to transform that place into a dream job for the next superintendent. Every situation is what you make it. So, I called the contact for the superintendent role. To my surprise, I had entertained him and a group of members on a past visit to Snowdrift Golf Club. I had played golf with them, served them lunch, and helped them with everything else they needed for the day. You never know when your past will come back to help you! The hardest part about applying for these jobs was getting an interview, and now I had an in. I knew that meant an opportunity.

I did a quick site tour before my interview. I met Tim, the Director of Golf, whom I would report to. Tim seemed like a great guy. He showed me the facility and then left while I toured the course with the assistant superintendent. Once I got home from the course tour, I told Molly that Tim would be leaving shortly. He didn't tell me so, but I've been around the industry a long time and can tell when the job has beat someone into making a change. That sucked because Tim was awesome. I was right; he left the following year.

My interview strategy was simple: prepare in advance by learning everything possible about the facility, and be myself (naturally aggressive) during the interview. I would attack the interview like I attack each day. If they didn't like it, they wouldn't like me, and it wouldn't work out anyway. I had nothing to lose. My current job was great, and I had told my boss, Brian, about every step in the process. The guys interviewing me were a bunch of dudes I thought I could get along with.

The first two interviews flowed well. What I believe set them apart from past interviews was I didn't go in with a set agenda. I didn't overthink or try to force anything. I just let the conversation flow naturally between the six to eight members present. I was invited back for a third interview. Everyone seemed excited when I sat down. Early in this interview, they let it slip I was everyone's number-one choice, which was great but not the best thing for their negotiating position. When they made me an official offer, I turned it down. When I turned down their second offer, they asked me to leave the room so they could discuss among themselves. They brought me back for a third offer, which was close to what I wanted, but I still turned it down. I wasn't desperate; I already had a great job, and for me to make the move, the salary had to be worth it. We ran out of time, so I left wondering if they would bend enough to make it work. Tim was the mediator for phone calls that night while negotiations continued. At 8:30 p.m. that night, we came to an agreement. I took the job.

I knew the first couple years were going to be rough, but I'm a firm believer in creating your own narrative. I knew I couldn't focus on any of the negative aspects I had heard about the club. All I had to do was improve the playing conditions and trust everything would fall into place. I was going to take this job that many mocked—some friends and colleagues couldn't believe I had accepted it!—and make it into one of the best jobs in the Chicagoland area. It wouldn't happen overnight, but if I could gain the trust of the membership, I could make it happen.

First, I needed to align with the crew I'd been hearing horror stories about. Even the Deer Hills interviewers kept bringing up all the trouble the past guy had with employees. I assured them it was not an issue. I wasn't too worried because I'd been changing the cultures of crews since my first year out of college. I was tossed into the fire at Colt and had refined the craft of winning over employees each year since. Plus, no place I ever worked would be a bigger dumpster fire for employees than Snowdrift. And there, my pool of potential employees was a fraction of the pool I now had in the Chicagoland area. Plus, my new employer told me in the interviews they wanted to take care of the good employees they had on staff. They were willing to pay more or do this or that to make employees happy—a tool I didn't possess at Snowdrift. I told them how I recruited crew members in middle-of-nowhere cornfield country. I took my guys out to lunch at local businesses and left job ads where they would allow. I took job postings to local gyms and YMCAs. I made sure my information was available wherever potential employees might frequent often. I successfully recruited as many employees as the course owner would allow at Snowdrift. They didn't all work out, but eventually, we had a decent crew, and I created a pipeline that paid dividends year after year.

To my surprise, I met the employees at Deer Hills, and they all seemed great, besides those in a few of the leadership positions. Most guys had worked there for over ten years, and a couple had worked there nearly thirty. A few who had quit during past seasons due to disagreements with the last superintendent even came back to give it another chance with a new superintendent. But no matter how great a crew is, incorporating change is always difficult. People are hesitant to leave their comfort zones. It's hard for them to see the big picture right away, especially when they feel frustrated from change. What I've found works well in these transitions is to connect with the few vocal leaders on staff. So, I communicated with those leaders in great detail about what I was trying to accomplish. After they started seeing improvements on the course, everything began to make sense to them. Many of my guys talked about feeling beaten down during past seasons. Now, they were seeing positive, efficient changes and getting great feedback on the course from members. Everything was different. That in-season beat-down feeling was gone for them. They started feeling positive about their work. Even the members noticed and kept asking how I made the guys work so hard for me. It was simple: I set the example, listened to them, and did what I could to take care of them. You're only as good as your crew, and I had lucked out. By making a few minor changes, I was able to create one of the best crews I have ever been a part of. They all took so much pride in their work; it was easy after they bought into my vision. The only other crew I'd worked with that came close to these guys was the crew at the Liberty Club. What those two crews had in common was a great foreman and guys who had been there a long time.

Another thing I worked to change was the perception of Deer Hills. I kept hearing the same narrative of bad finances and unpleasant members and homeowners. I had to attack that narrative with tenacity. I was determined to will a more positive narrative into existence. I created a positive vibe and was relentless in turning up the buzz around the course. When sales reps stopped by, I sang the praises of my membership and how supportive they were. I showed them all the projects we were doing and the resources the club was putting back into the facility. Then I'd jokingly remind them about how bad of a place this was to work while wearing the biggest smile you've ever seen.

It wasn't easy, but I created the job and work environment I desired. I'm still trying to get everything in order at the course while balancing work and family. My lifestyle is a superintendent lifestyle, but I want to incorporate my family into that lifestyle more moving forward. And I will because I am prioritizing that goal.

CHAPTER 21

WEDDING BELLS AND FAMILY FALLOUT

Molly and me on our wedding day.

A TRUE TEST OF MY RELATIONSHIP WITH MOLLY CAME
when I first started at Deer Hills. The commute from my house
was one hour and thirteen minutes in the morning and one
hour and forty-five minutes in the afternoon due to traffic. Even
though I had renovated my house for a year to get it exactly
how I wanted it, we decided to move closer to my new job. I
was finishing painting and hanging bathroom mirrors the day
before we listed the house. At least I got experience renovating a house! We rented an apartment near my work while we
looked for a house we liked. We moved from my dream home
to a two-bedroom apartment that constantly smelled like cigarette smoke because of our neighbors. Oh, how fun it was. But
Molly and I happily made it through those living arrangements.
I knew if we made it through that, our future would be fine.

Molly got together with all the friends she grew up with from
her hometown once a year for "Friendsgiving" in November.
Her good friend Will hosted each year. I wanted to give Molly
a special proposal, and I figured what could be more special
for her than sharing that moment with her closest friends?
I planned it for nearly a year. I was completely clueless as I
walked into a store to purchase her ring. The jeweler might as
well have been speaking a foreign language as he talked about
the quality of diamonds. I nervously picked one I thought Molly
would like and got out of the store as quickly as possible. Next, I
ran my plan to propose at Friendsgiving by Will, and he eagerly
agreed. Then, I just had to keep the ring hidden from Molly for
four months before I could pop the question. In the meantime,
I asked her father for his approval. He gave his blessing, and
we shared a drink or two in celebration.

The night finally came, and Molly had no clue what I was
up to. As all her friends stood in a circle at Will's house, about
to say grace before dinner, Will passed the floor to me. I told

everyone I had a question to ask Molly and dropped to one knee. Her eyes filled with tears, and one hand covered her face. The room got loud with applause. I couldn't hear her answer. So, I stood up to hug her and quietly asked her, "Did you say yes?" She had. Tears of joy ran down my face. Everything had gone perfectly.

We began planning the wedding, creating a list of friends and family we wanted to share our day with. I called Uncle Noah, excited to tell him about the engagement. But the conversation took a wrong turn when he asked if I had told my mom yet. I told him I hadn't, and then he asked if she was going to be invited to the wedding. I told him no. Although she was out of jail and doing well, my relationship with her had run its course, and I didn't feel comfortable having her there.

When this conversation happened, the only time I saw my mom was during trips home for Christmas, the one event everyone in my family attended each year. We would meet at her house with my little brother, exchange presents, pick up Grandma Cathy, and head over to Grandpa Jones's house. My favorite moments were spending time with Gunner and Grandma Cathy before we went to visit with the rest of the family. It gave us more one-on-one time to catch up. It was the silver lining to spending time with my mom. I just didn't feel comfortable around her.

After I told my uncle I would not be inviting my mom to the wedding, his tone changed. He told me I needed to invite her. He began to give me advice, as he always had, but this subject was different. In the middle of his speech, I stopped him. I said, "Noah, this is something you don't understand. You are telling me how to feel about a situation you are unaware of, and I know you're telling me this because you love me, but these types of conversations can tear relationships apart." My brief interruption did not stop him. He continued telling me stories from his past when he regretted not making up with someone. But his stories were not similar to mine in any way. Not once did he mention a decade of child neglect or hearing his mom say he ruined her life, making him feel worthless every day afterward. I went from being excited to share happy news to just feeling sad. I had wanted to share my joy with someone I looked up to, someone I wanted to be like when I was younger, someone I thought understood me. But he was totally against me.

Normally, when my mom called or texted me, I didn't reply. But the next time she called, I answered; I knew I needed to tell her about my engagement myself. The first thing she said was that Noah told her I was getting married. She was angry and wanted to know why she couldn't come to the wedding. She asked whether or not my dad was invited. I informed her he was, which only infuriated her more. We had never spoken about the past, so she might not have understood the trauma she had caused. She said she thought I was trying to get back at her by not inviting her. I explained I didn't feel comfortable around her, and I didn't want to feel uncomfortable on my wedding day. I wanted to enjoy my wedding.

She kept pushing me to explain but wouldn't accept my answers. I personally didn't think I needed to explain anything. My wedding wasn't about her, but she continued to push. I finally told her, "Mom, somehow I was naive enough to believe you weren't doing drugs while I was growing up. Even not knowing about the drugs, I remember being fourteen years old and telling one of my friends that I didn't have any respect for you. I didn't say it in anger. It just casually came up in our conversation. I didn't know why at the time, but looking back, I see all the times you chose drugs over me. How are we supposed to have a relationship? And then, you brought Gunner into an environment where you were making meth. Any chance of salvaging a meaningful relationship with you was over at that point. Seeing you put someone else in harm's way, someone who couldn't do anything to protect himself, ruined that chance."

Even then, she continued accusing me of making a deliberate attack against her. I had to stop her. I told her I was sorry and said goodbye. Once off the phone, I just shook my head. As always, she thought everyone was against her and took no accountability for the destruction she caused. She made me this way. She is the one who chose drugs over my well-being. Raising me in that environment was not going to produce a normal kid.

An hour or two later, my mom's sister called me. We had talked maybe five times in my entire life, and I had not seen or spoken to her in years. She proceeded to tell me my mom should be at my wedding and I needed therapy. She said my mom was similar to my grandmother, more of a friend to her children than a mother. My aunt claimed she was able to overcome that and accept her mother for who she was, and so should I. I told her my situation was a little different. Just as in my conversations with my uncle and mom, I never once raised my voice with my aunt. I calmly explained I wasn't going to talk badly about my mom. I had accepted what happened in the past and moved on without her long ago.

Molly had listened to the entire conversation and was more fired up than I was. I was just sad and disappointed. I felt like my family was more against me now than ever over something they didn't understand. My aunt and I talked in circles a little while longer. I was thinking, *You've got to be kidding. This lady does not know me, and now she is telling me I need therapy and how I should feel about my mom?* Finally, I decided to end the conversation. I calmly said goodbye and hung up. I can't blame my family for what they don't know. The only thing that did get me fired up was my aunt telling me I needed therapy when she knew nothing about me. But I kept my composure. The situation wasn't an angry one; it was just sad. I was excited to share my engagement with my family, but it went in a different direction.

The best conversation I had about the wedding was with my dad. He was happy for me, which I enjoyed. Of course, he too asked if my mom was going. When I said no, he told me, "You need to invite your mother."

Instead of responding the way I had with the rest of my family, I decided to use an example. My dad loves his little seventeen-year-old dog named Rex (who seems like he's one hundred years old) more than anything. So, I said, "Dad, let's say a dog was neglected by his owner for a decade. Then that dog is cast out or escapes and finds a new family who loves him. The dog is doing great, gets back to a normal weight, and isn't skittish anymore. He is living a great life. Would you force that dog to be around the person who neglected him for so long? The answer is no. So why would it be different with a human?" He seemed to understand, and our conversation moved on to another topic.

Uncle Noah called me a couple days later. He avoided the subject of my wedding for the most part, but he did comment about how I was making a mistake and how good my mom was doing now. Then, right before we hung up, he said, "Oh, and I respect my sister." That was just another unnecessary dig on circumstances he didn't understand.

During all of the conversations with my family, I told each of them that time could change everything. I was never going to totally write off my mom. Maybe we would reconcile in the future, but I wasn't there yet. I don't know if I'll ever be, and that's okay.

The crazy part was I didn't feel anything toward her. No hate, no anger, no joy—nothing. She was just a person from my past. Our relationship ran a screwed-up course, and not every movie has a happy ending. I compared my situation to the TV show *Game of Thrones*. I would argue that the show was ruined by what felt like a forced neat-and-tidy ending wrapped up with balloons and bows. After watching the gritty and often tragic themes from previous seasons, many fans felt the integrity of the show was lost at the end. Too many writers and showrunners got involved with too many opinions, and *Game of Thrones* lost its roots that everyone loved so much. I wasn't going to make that mistake. I will not force a renewed, insincere relationship with my mother to please others.

Here's another example of fiction imitating real life. Have you ever seen the 2007 movie *Gone Baby Gone*? To summarize, the main character, Patrick, has a choice to make: report information he found that puts a young girl back in the custody of her drug-addicted mom, or don't report and allow the innocent little girl to live with a family who will love and take care of her. During Patrick's investigation, the mom promises she'll never go out again if she gets her daughter back. Patrick chooses to report and put the child back in the mother's home. The movie ends with the little girl's mom going out while Patrick babysits the kid, facing the consequences of his choice: he lost his girlfriend because she disagreed with his decision, and he realizes how much he set back this child in life. In my opinion, no way in hell should that innocent, little girl have been allowed to live with her mother while she's an addict.

I wish some of my family would watch that movie to give them a glimpse into what it was like for me growing up. When you live with an addict, everything revolves around the addiction. Just like the mom in the movie left her little girl in a car for hours while she went inside somewhere to drink and do drugs, my mom did the same; that was a constant during my childhood. I was set up to fail. I had countless obstacles to overcome, and I did. I now live an extremely happy and healthy life.

Therapy probably would've helped me when I was growing up, but then I would have run the risk of being put on prescription drugs for anxiety, depression, and ADD and being suicidal. These days, the majority of doctors don't show you how to move on; they just treat your symptoms. I think putting a kid on drugs at a young age is like trying to pin the tail on a donkey blindfolded. A kid's body chemistry and hormones are constantly changing. Once a kid begins taking these types of drugs, any drugs, their body recalibrates, making it that much harder to get back to neutral. I actually believe I'm lucky my mom was too preoccupied with drugs to worry about me. I even believe I was lucky to play football and have that back and brain injury and that my dad kicked me out of the house. All those experiences changed my perspective. They showed me I was the one who needed to figure things out for myself.

Ultimately, Molly and I had a wonderful wedding without my mother present. While other people in my family might want to act like a "normal" family from a movie, I think the great therapist and author Catherine Gildiner said it best in her book *Good Morning, Monster*: "Normal is just a setting on a washing machine."

CHAPTER 22

THE DEMON REARS ITS HEAD

LIFE MOVED ON, AND IT WASN'T LONG BEFORE MOLLY WAS pregnant. She ended up having a C-section after trying to be induced for nearly eight hours. While she was on the operating table, I was draped behind her, holding both her hands. We could tell it was getting close, and then, we heard our baby cry out. Hearing my little girl, Darby, cry for the first time was a moment I'll never forget. It was the most wonderful sound I've heard in my life. We grasped each other more tightly and wept joyful tears. As soon as our tears subsided, Molly surprisingly said, "Let's have another child." Then she kept asking for her baby. Watching her motherly instincts kick in was amazing.

Darby

Once we got home from the hospital, everything was fine for the first couple weeks. I was doing really well taking care of our baby. After all, my mom had Gunner when I was nine years old, and I did everything for him. I fed him bottles, changed his diapers, and watched him. This prior experience helped me feel quite comfortable taking care of Darby.

But, after a few weeks, things began to change. The sound of

Darby crying uncontrollably took me back to watching my little brother when he was little and trying to console him. I was supposed to be watching him while my mom was locked in her room. He would scream, cry, beat on her door, and ask for his mom. I would do everything possible to keep this from happening. When it went on for too long, my mom would come out and yell at me for not taking care of him. Then she would lock herself back in her room, and the cycle would start again. Just as I felt scared and overwhelmed by Gunner's crying and the next lashing out from my mom back then, I felt those exact same emotions now.

The sound of crying also took me back to when I was around eleven years old. At that time, I was constantly thinking of ways to end my life in such a way that I would not be able to back out of at the last minute. Experiencing suicidal thoughts while I was watching an uncontrollable child had me near the breaking point. My thoughts of self-harm would sometimes shift to Gunner. I wanted to physically harm him the same way I wanted to end my life. Each time I heard Darby cry, I felt like I was back in that apartment, pulling my hair out and beating my head against the wall to find relief from reality in pain. Remembering the dark thoughts I had about an innocent child who just wanted his mom was scary, especially when I looked at my little girl. I loved her more than anything, but I felt like a scared kid. When she cried, she was just a baby doing what a baby does, but I couldn't help feeling like she was afraid of me or didn't like me. My thoughts wouldn't stop. I wondered, *Could she somehow tell I used to want to physically hurt another child? Does she sense I'm a bad person? Does she hate being around me?* I began to become a prisoner of my own mind again. People who go through trauma as children never get rid of it completely. No matter how good of a spot they put themselves in, the trauma is always in the background, waiting to come out.

Darby and Cori

I didn't recognize what was happening right away. The first thing I noticed was that Darby's cries started sounding dull to my ears. Then, one day, when I was rocking Darby in her room, I noticed the walls looked strange. Though it was a sunny day, with light shining in at different angles, the colors of the walls and my surroundings were dull and lifeless, just like the sound of Darby's cries. It finally clicked. I was back in a world of no emotions. I realized I'd been here before: depression. I had bypassed all the other signs leading up to that point. I had lost my appetite and was down more than ten pounds. I had been having nightmares about my mom and my childhood that were so disturbing I'd wake up and be too emotionally charged to fall back asleep. When Molly asked me a week earlier if stuttering ran in my family, I couldn't control my emotions. I had to step away and gather myself while crying uncontrollably. When she came to check on me, I blurted out, "Why didn't someone get me out of there? Everyone knew something was wrong. They got Gunner out, but what about me?"

Once I understood I was dealing with depression again (possibly postpartum depression caused by PTSD), I knew I needed to tell Molly. It was hard to do because I wanted to be her rock, her constant. She was already dealing with so much from breastfeeding and trying to get Darby to latch correctly, not to mention her body was recovering from the C-section. The last thing I wanted to do was give her something else to worry about, but I knew we had to have the conversation. I had told Molly I had a big part in raising Gunner, but I had never told her about my thoughts of physical harm. I started by telling her I was dealing with something a little extra—a little more than the lack of sleep from a newborn while working seven days a week. I then told her everything, and she was very appreciative of my honesty. She said it all started to make sense: why I wasn't eating as much, why I wasn't there mentally, and why I had become more emotional. I reassured her I was still in control and had dealt with this before in much worse circumstances; I knew what I needed to do. I promised I would keep her updated and let her know if I felt like I was losing control.

Once your head gets in a depressed space, it's hard to pull yourself out. Your mind drifts and wants to take you down some dark roads. To recover, you must first be aware of your depression. Once I recognized the signs and vocalized what was happening, I knew how to pull myself out. How did I have that confidence? Because I had done it before. The only thing I didn't know was how long it would take. Depression has its own timeline, and trauma from your past can be triggered by stuff that's out of your control. It's important to know that and accept it. Trauma never goes away. Figuring out how to cope is your duty to yourself.

The first thing I did was narrow my focus. I had to focus on myself; I couldn't carry others' burdens. My diet at the time was okay but not great. So, I started eating cleaner, and I didn't drink alcohol for a while. Eating cleaner meant eating only foods approved by the Whole 30 diet. Gut health is a leading factor in determining mood.[2] I also needed to engage in more physical activity. Exercise was found to be as effective as anti-depressants and doesn't negatively affect your sleep like SSRIs. On the weekends, I only worked half days, so working out both those days was no problem. But during the week was tough. When I got home from work, I liked to give Molly a break from watching the baby. Taking care of a baby is super stressful; she needed a few hours each day for herself. Working out before work wasn't an option because I started work at 5:00 a.m. I came up with an efficient solution: running. I would get home from work, toss on my shoes, and hit the pavement. I'd run for forty-five minutes and be done. Then, I'd have plenty of time to watch the baby so Molly could have a break.

Did changing my diet and exercising more cure my depression right away? Of course not. But I knew if I was consistent, eventually, colors and emotions would come back to my life.

---

2 Studies showing food interventions can treat depression and anxiety can be found at SMILEs by Felice Jacka, AMMEND by Jessica Bayes, and HELFIMED by Natalie Parletta.

Each day, I was tired from lack of sleep and beat down from the demands of work, but I knew with 100 percent confidence I would be okay if I stayed the course. After a few weeks, my thoughts became clear, and Darby's cry sounded like a wonderful baby's cry again. I checked in with Molly during this time to let her know how I was doing. I knew I was not out of the woods yet, but I was moving in the right direction. I wanted to be able to enjoy my time with my beautiful little girl again. That desire was great motivation, but was it enough? I knew what having an absent parent does to a kid because I lived it. I would rather die than fail to do my duties as a father with this innocent little girl. It took a total of five or six weeks before I felt completely comfortable again, but my determination to not repeat my parents' mistakes is what drove me past the finish line.

Darby and me

Before my experience with Darby, I thought I was in a good spot mentally. I came to realize that no matter what I do, some things are out of my control, and that's okay. Trauma never leaves. You better have a system in place to combat mental setbacks when they happen because they will. Always remember you are not the only one battling these issues. Don't be too proud to let someone know what's going on. You can't start recovering until you recognize the issue.

CHAPTER 23

WITH HARD WORK, THERE ARE NO LIMITS

IT WAS FRUSTRATING FOR ME THAT MY FAMILY COULDN'T understand my situation. It was especially concerning when my aunt told me I needed therapy. If I was unhappy, ashamed of my past, or had issues that kept me from living a healthy life, I would look into all options, including therapy; but that wasn't the case. I would not change a single thing that happened to me growing up. I embrace it. It gives me strength and helps me keep my integrity. I love my past and the perspective it gives me while navigating life. What I went through battle-tested me and made me find artillery to fight back and take control in life.

Accepting my past did not happen overnight, but I do remember the night it started. A few close friends and I were at Quinn's house in the months after my mom went to jail. The Quinns had a good amount of land out in the middle of nowhere in Kentucky. About one hundred yards below their house was what we called the party barn because it was where we partied in high school. But this event wasn't a party. We were sitting around the campfire, and someone brought up my mom going to jail. They asked if I knew anything about what happened. I hadn't really talked about it before, but a range of emotions had been building up.

Up until that night, I pretended to my friends that everything bad rolled off me with a bullshit smile. I was convinced they looked at me differently because I grew up with a meth addict. I told them I didn't know about it. I felt like something was off growing up, but I didn't know my mom was on meth or making meth in our backyard. What kid could think that about their mother? Growing up in that environment was my normal.

That night, around the campfire, I couldn't hold back the tears any longer. I told my friends about all my concerns. I asked if they looked at me differently knowing my mom was a meth addict. Every person there was understanding and reassured me they saw me in a more positive light after my mom went to jail. After that, my tears continued, but this time, they came from joy. My friends, whom I considered family, all accepted me. A huge weight was lifted. Being open and sharing with my friends freed me from the burden of shame I had been carrying, which had been affecting me in a negative way.

This was the start of me accepting myself. I began to be more open. A part of the process was realizing I can't control what people think of me. All that is just outside noise. Life is hard and unforgiving. I know I can't let anything, including other people's opinions, hold me back. I've battled too hard throughout life to let anyone else affect my self-image. Worrying about and trying to control what someone thinks about me does not affect that person at all; it only hurts me and lets the demons win.

Learning to control the noise and increase my self-worth

was a long process. I lucked into finding some tools that help. Working out has been a constant since I started playing football. Then, after my back injury, I realized I needed to work out to alleviate my chronic pain. I'm not a fast learner, but I eventually figured out I was much more mentally stable when I worked out. Having bigger muscles in itself is not what improves my mental health; it's about showing myself that I can fight back against my mind when it doesn't want to do something that's uncomfortable. Your mind knows every trick in the book to talk you out of something. When that happens, I know I need to take control and see it through. It could be as small as just going to work out that day or not eating my weight in pizza. It's about controlling those urges and adding stressors by strain to show who's really in control. Just compiling little wins like that helps me gain confidence and increase my chances of success in larger goals. Doing something your mind told you not to do while under strain is how you strengthen your mind and take control. It's about consistently being able to persevere and watch all the roadblocks your mind has built crumble away. It's about opening the door and letting confidence control your life. The path is never a straight line. Life, injuries, or lack of focus are always going to try and slow your growth, but just know if you remain consistent while embracing the process, you can overcome all obstacles.

Another tool I use is eating clean. What this means is following a whole-foods diet. When I started doing CrossFit, I learned about the paleo diet and lifestyle. Once I strictly followed this way of eating for four weeks, I noticed a change in my energy levels and sharpness. I was less bogged down throughout the day. It helped with my confidence, enabled me to start making larger strides in my profession, and stabilized my mood. Many people don't realize how much what they put in their bodies affects them. They don't know how much processed foods inflame the body. As the body tries to combat inflammation each day, it can't focus on recovery. Most people walk around in an inflamed state their entire lives without knowing it. I didn't understand that until I read the book *Whole 30,* which is what I now base my eating habits on. I strongly recommend everyone read it. It could be life changing. Many ailments you've been told are out of your control are actually caused by your diet. Some ailments this guide claims to cure are allergies, arthritis, asthma, ADD, celiac disease, Crohn's disease, diabetes, depression, fibromyalgia, GERD, high blood pressure/cholesterol, inflammatory bowel disease, lupus, migraines, thyroid disorders, skin blemishes, low energy, dull mental focus, and difficulty sleeping, to name a few.

Once a year, I strictly follow the Whole 30 diet. Then, I do mini Whole 30 stints throughout the year, as needed. When I do this, I know I'm at my strongest and can take deep dives mentally. Thinking about hard topics is not comfortable, but I reevaluate everything, including my mom, family, friends, jobs, and goals. I bring everything into focus and decide where changes are needed. I also have tough conversations with myself, my family, and my friends. If tension has been building up with someone in my life, I have a grown-up conversation with that person. Letting things build and keeping them inside is not healthy. I did that for too long and don't have time for it anymore.

Everyone is always looking for someone or something else to give them strength. Once you're able to look inward and gather strength from within yourself, you've begun to figure life out. I've been developing my mental strength for nearly two decades by putting in the work and committing to doing whatever is necessary for my job and myself, and I don't accept any excuses. That's why my aunt saying I need therapy rubbed me the wrong way. I have invested in myself for so long and figured out how to live as the best version of myself. Now, I have a beautiful wife and daughter that I'm able to be there for. I give them myself in a way that didn't feel possible years ago. I've built myself into a person who can be vulnerable, giving, loving, and accepting of love.

Though I worked hard to get myself to a healthy place, the backlash I felt from my family and mom still surprised me. When something like that happens, you find out if you're really comfortable with who you are. If you listen to my mom talk these days, you'll hear how she excelled at being a mother. My family thinks I should accept her back into my life because she's my mom. But the person who raised me wasn't a mom. It wasn't even human, it was a drug-addicted monster that fed on destruction. Her clawing her face off for endless hours in the mirror only to pop out and yell at me covered in bloody, pus-filled boils didn't allow us to develop that relationship. She was an addict with an addiction that trumped all. It's hard for others to see that in their daughter, sister, or friend because they didn't have to live with her addiction like I did every day. If you are in my position, do not be blindsided if others don't understand where you're coming from. I want you to know it's okay to feel the way you feel. Remember, normal is just a setting on a washing machine.

In this book, I've laid out what helped me deal with my past mental and physical issues. I've gone to uncomfortable places time and time again to help build my character and to allow me to let you know you're not alone. I'm not anywhere close to perfect and never will be, but I'm always battling and trying to do better.

I have one challenge for you: be the one who stops the cycle of addiction in your family, as I stopped it in mine.

My little girl will never have to deal with the neglect, trauma, and abuse that comes from being raised by a meth addict. Stopping that cycle is insanely hard; you have to endure more than you thought possible for a lifetime. But it can be done, and it is worth it.

My little brother was not so lucky. Addiction consumed him; he has not escaped its grasp yet. One of his drugs of choice is meth. I'm scared shitless every day that I'm going to get a phone call telling me he overdosed or took a batch laced with fentanyl. He's such a good, bright young man. Witnessing his generational addiction is devastating.

Maybe you can stop the cycle! Take hope from my story. Try some of my strategies or develop your own to take back control of your life. Never give up fighting for a better life. You are worth it.

Milton Keynes UK
Ingram Content Group UK Ltd.
UKHW010849280324
440101UK00001B/100